Reasoning *and* Sense Making *in the* Mathematics Classroom

Grades 3–5

Michael T. Battista

Series Editor
The Ohio State University
Columbus, Ohio

NATIONAL COUNCIL OF
TEACHERS OF MATHEMATICS

www.nctm.org/more4u
Access code: RMC14311

Copyright © 2017 by
The National Council of Teachers of Mathematics, Inc.
1906 Association Drive, Reston, VA 20191-1502
(703) 620-9840; (800) 235-7566; www.nctm.org
All rights reserved

Library of Congress Cataloging-in-Publication Data

Names: Battista, Michael T. | Baek, Jae-Meen. | Cramer, Kathleen. |Blanton,
    Maria L.
Title: Reasoning and sense making in the elementary grades, grades 3-5 /
    Michael T. Battista, Jae Meen Baek, Kathleen Cramer, Maria Blanton.
Description: Reston, VA : National Council of Teachers of Mathematics,
[2016]
    | Includes bibliographical references. | Description based on print
    version record and CIP data provided by publisher; resource not viewed.
Identifiers: LCCN 2016017652 (print) | LCCN 2016013208 (ebook) | ISBN
    9780873538787 () | ISBN 9780873537032 (pbk.)
Subjects: LCSH: Mathematics--Study and teaching (Elementary)--United
States.
    | Problem solving.
Classification: LCC QA13 (print) | LCC QA13 .B38 2016 (ebook) | DDC
    372.7/049--dc23
LC record available at https://lccn.loc.gov/2016017652

Cover Image: ©Shutterstock/new year

The National Council of Teachers of Mathematics is the public voice
of mathematics education, supporting teachers to ensure equitable
mathematics learning of the highest quality for each and every student
through vision, leadership, professional development, and research.

Printed in the United States of America

Contents

Preface v

Mathematical Reasoning and Sense Making............... 1

1   Michael T. Battista, The Ohio State University,
       Columbus, Ohio

Numerical Reasoning: Making Sense of Numbers and
Operations through Multiplication in Grades 3–5 23

2   Jae Meen Baek, Illinois State University
       Normal, Illinois

Numerical Reasoning: Number and Operations
with Fractions.. 43

3   Kathleen Cramer, University of Minnesota,
       St. Paul, Minn.

Algebraic Reasoning in Grades 3–5 67

4   Maria Blanton, TERC, Cambridge, Mass.

Understanding and Developing Intermediate Students'
Reasoning and Sense Making in Decomposing Shapes
to Reason About Area and Volume Measurement..........103

5   Michael T. Battista, The Ohio State University,
       Columbus, Ohio

Appendix A: Abbreviated List of the *Common Core
State Standards for Mathematics* Standards for
Mathematical Practice 141

Appendix B: Abbreviated List of the National Council
of Teachers of Mathematics *Principles and Standards
for School Mathematics* Process Standards 145

Preface

This is the second of the three-book series *Reasoning and Sense Making in the Mathematics Classroom*. The books maintain the National Council of Teachers of Mathematics' (NCTM) focus on teaching that promotes and supports mathematical reasoning and sense making, and they emphasize implementation of the Common Core State Standards for Mathematics (CCSSM) Standards for Mathematical Practice (SMP; NGA Center and CCSSO 2010) and the Process Standards (PS) from NCTM's *Principles and Standards for School Mathematics* (*Principles and Standards*; NCTM 2000). To illustrate the nature of mathematical reasoning and sense making in prekindergarten–grade 8 and the critical role that reasoning and sense making play in learning and using mathematics, these books show—through student and classroom vignettes as well as instructional tasks—how instruction can support students in their development of reasoning and sense making. (All student and classroom dialogues in this book are either edited versions of actual student/classroom dialogue or composites of dialogue from research and classroom observation. Student names have been changed throughout.)

Throughout this book, research on student learning is used to help teachers understand, monitor, and guide the development of students' reasoning and sense making about core ideas in elementary school mathematics. Research on teaching and learning mathematics, as cited in the chapters, is the basis of all the discussions and recommendations in this book. To illuminate the connection between reasoning and mathematical content, all three books concentrate on sense making as it is implemented for specific content areas in prekindergarten–grade 8 mathematics learning. In this book, we focus on number and operations, fractions, algebraic reasoning, and decomposing and composing geometric shapes.

Michael Battista opens the book with a discussion on the nature of reasoning and sense making in grades 3–5 and why they are critically important in the development of mathematical thinking. He illustrates the nature of children's mathematical reasoning with examples of students attempting to make sense of the division of fractions and the concept of length.

In chapter 2, Jae Meen Baek examines student strategies that exemplify conceptually sound reasoning and sense making in the context of multiplication word problems. She discusses how instruction can support students' growth in this reasoning, as well as the critical topic of properties of numbers that underlie reasoning about multiplication.

In chapter 3, Kathleen Cramer describes how students in grades 3–5 extend their understanding of number to include fractions and how they can build reasoning and sense making for fractions through explorations of different representations, such as physical materials, pictures, and story contexts.

In chapter 4, Maria Blanton discusses the nature of early algebraic reasoning and provides research-based descriptions of how children in grades 3–5 reason algebraically. She also addresses how classroom practice can support this reasoning and how mathematical content in the elementary grades can integrate algebra in appropriate ways.

In Chapter 5, Michael Battista discusses practices and processes connected to reasoning about geometric decomposition and structuring as applied to arrays of squares and cubes and to area and volume problems. He also examines a learning progression for the development of such reasoning and the instructional practices that are consistent with this learning progression.

For your convenience in following discussions of practices and standards cited within the text, two appendices consisting of abbreviated and labeled versions of the CCSSM Standards for Mathematical Practice (SMP) and the Process Standards (PS) from NCTM's *Principles and Standards* are included in the book. You can also access the appendixes, along with other resources, by visiting NCTM's More4U website (nctm.org/more4u). The access code can be found on the title page of this book.

Mathematical Reasoning and Sense Making[1]

Michael T. Battista

Reasoning and sense making are the foundation of mathematical competence and proficiency, and their absence leads to failure and disengagement in mathematics instruction. Thus, developing students' capabilities with reasoning and sense making should be the primary goal of mathematics instruction. In order to achieve this goal, all mathematics classes should provide ongoing opportunities for students to implement these processes.

What are mathematical reasoning and sense making? *Reasoning* is the process of manipulating and analyzing objects, representations, diagrams, symbols, or statements to draw conclusions based on evidence or assumptions. *Sense making* is the process of understanding ideas and concepts in order to correctly identify, describe, explain, and apply them. Genuine sense making makes mathematical ideas "feel" clear, logical, valid, or obvious. The moment of sense making is often signaled by exclamations such as "Aha!" "I get it!" or "Oh, I see!"

Why Focus on Reasoning and Sense Making?

Reasoning and sense making are critical in mathematics learning because students who genuinely make sense of mathematical ideas can apply them in problem solving and unfamiliar situations and can use them as a foundation for future learning. Even with mathematical skills, "[i]n order to learn skills so that they are remembered, can be applied when they are needed, and can be adjusted to solve new problems, they must be learned with understanding [i.e., they must make sense]" (Hiebert et al. 1997, p. 6).

Sense making is also important because it is an intellectually satisfying experience, and not making sense is frustrating (Hiebert et al. 1997). Students who achieve genuine understanding and sense making of mathematics are likely to stay engaged in learning it. Students who fail to understand and make sense of mathematical ideas and instead resort to rote learning will eventually experience continued failure and withdraw from mathematics learning.

Understanding How Students Think

An abundance of research describing how students learn mathematics indicates that effective mathematics instruction is based on the following three principles (Battista 2001; Bransford, Brown, and Cocking 1999; De Corte, Greer, and Verschaffel 1996; Greeno, Collins, and Resnick 1996; Hiebert and Carpenter 1992; Lester 1994; NRC 1989; Prawat 1999; Romberg 1992; Schoenfeld 1994; Steffe and Kieren 1994):

1. To genuinely understand mathematical ideas, students must construct these ideas for themselves as they intentionally try to make sense of situations; their success in constructing the meaning of new mathematical ideas is determined by their preexisting knowledge and types of reasoning and by their commitment to making personal sense of those ideas.

2. To be effective, mathematics teaching must carefully guide and support students as they attempt to construct personally meaningful mathematical ideas in the context of problem solving, inquiry, and student discussion of multiple problem-solving strategies. This sense-making and discussion approach to teaching can increase equitable student access to powerful mathematical ideas, as long as it regularly uses embedded formative assessment to determine the amount of guidance each student needs. (Some students construct ideas quite well with little guidance other than well-chosen sequences of problems; other students need more direct guidance, sometimes in the form of explicit description.)

3. To effectively guide and support students in constructing the meaning of mathematical ideas, instruction must be derived from research-based descriptions of how students develop reasoning about particular mathematical topics (such as those given in research-based learning progressions).

Consistent with this view on learning and teaching, professional recommendations and research suggest that mathematics teachers should possess extensive research-based knowledge of students' mathematical thinking (An, Kulm, and Wu 2004; Carpenter and Fennema 1991; Clarke and Clarke 2004; Fennema and Franke 1992; Saxe et al. 2001; Schifter 1998; Tirosh 2000). Teachers should "be aware of learners' prior knowledge about particular topics and how that knowledge is organized and structured" (Borko and Putnam 1995, p. 42). And because numerous researchers have found that students' development of understanding of particular mathematical ideas can be characterized in terms of developmental sequences or *learning progressions* (e.g., Battista and Clements 1996; Battista et al. 1998; Cobb and Wheatley 1988; Steffe 1992; van Hiele 1986), teachers must understand these learning progressions. They must understand "the general stages that students pass through in acquiring the concepts and procedures in the domain, the processes that are used to solve different problems at each stage, and the nature of the knowledge that underlies these processes" (Carpenter and Fennema 1991, p. 11). Research clearly shows that teacher use of such knowledge improves students' learning (Fennema and Franke 1992; Fennema et al. 1996). "There is a good deal of evidence that learning is enhanced when teachers pay attention to the knowledge and beliefs that learners bring to a learning task, use this knowledge as a starting point for new instruction, and monitor students' changing conceptions as instruction proceeds" (Bransford et al. 1999, p. 11).

Beyond understanding the development of students' mathematical reasoning, it is important to recognize that to be truly successful in learning mathematics, students must stay engaged in making personal sense of mathematical ideas. To stay engaged in mathematical sense making, students must be successful in solving *challenging but doable* problems. Such problems strike a delicate balance between involving students in the hard work of careful mathematical reasoning and having students succeed in problem solving, sense making, and learning. Keeping students successfully engaged in mathematical sense making requires us to understand each student's mathematical thinking well enough to continuously engage him or her in *successful* mathematical sense making. Furthermore, to pursue mathematical sense making during instruction, students must *believe*—based on past their experiences—that they are capable of making sense of mathematics. They must also believe that they are supposed to make sense of all the mathematical ideas discussed in their mathematics classes.

Finally, as part of the focus on reasoning and sense making in mathematics learning, students must adopt an inquiry disposition. Indeed, students learn more effectively when they adopt an active, questioning, inquiring frame of mind; such an inquiry disposition seems to be a natural characteristic of the mind's overall sense-making function (Ellis 1995; Feldman and Kalmar 1996).

Reaching All Students

The principled, research-based instruction described above not only helps all students maximize their learning but also benefits struggling students (Villasenor and Kepner 1993). In fact, this type of teaching supports all three tiers of Response to Intervention (RTI) instruction. For Tier 1, high-quality classroom instruction for all students, research-based instructional materials include extensive descriptions of the development of students' learning of particular mathematical topics. Research shows that teachers who understand such information about student learning teach in ways that produce greater student achievement. For Tier 2, research-based instruction enables teachers to better understand and monitor each student's mathematics learning through observation, embedded assessment, questioning, informal assessment during small-group work, and formative assessment. They can then choose instructional activities that meet their students' learning needs: whole-class tasks that benefit students at all levels or different tasks for small groups of students at the same level. For Tier 3, research-based assessments and learning progressions support student-specific instruction for struggling students so that they receive the long-term individualized instruction sequences they need.

Because extensive formative assessment is embedded in this type of teaching, support for its effectiveness also comes from research on the use of formative assessment, which indicates that formative assessment helps all students—and perhaps particularly struggling students—to produce significant learning gains, often reducing the learning gap between struggling students and their peers.

What Does Sense Making During Learning and Teaching Look Like?

The following two examples are illustrations of the development of students' reasoning and sense making about particular mathematical ideas. We examine obstacles to sense making, variations in student sense making, and how teaching can support sense making at various levels of sophistication.

Making Sense of Division of Fractions

To illustrate the nature of mathematical sense making, reasoning, and understanding, consider two different ways that students might reason about and make sense of the problem "What is $2\frac{1}{2}$ divided by $\frac{1}{4}$?" (Battista 1999). Many students solve this problem using the "invert and multiply" procedure they memorize and almost never understand:

$$2\frac{1}{2} \div \frac{1}{4} = \frac{5}{2} \times \frac{4}{1} = \frac{20}{2} = 10$$

They do not make conceptual sense of this procedure, and the only way they can justify it is by saying something like "That's the way my teacher taught me."

In contrast, students who have made sense of and understand division of fractions do not need a symbolic procedure to compute an answer to this problem. They can think about the symbolic problem physically as one that requires finding the number of pieces of size one-fourth that fit in a quantity of size two and one-half (see fig. 1.1). They reason that, since there are 4 fourths in each 1, and 2 fourths in $\frac{1}{2}$, there are 10 fourths in $2\frac{1}{2}$.

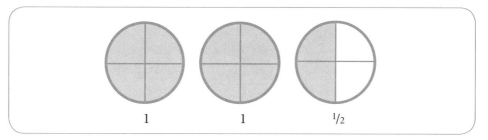

Fig. 1.1. Finding the number of fourths in $2^1/_2$

Furthermore, having this mental-model–based intuitive understanding of division of fractions can help students start to make personal sense of the symbolic algorithm. In the problem $2^1/_2 \div {}^1/_4$ why do we change division by $^1/_4$ to multiplication by 4? Because there are 4 fourths in each whole, to determine how many fourths are in the dividend $2^1/_2$, we must multiply the number of wholes in the dividend (including fractional parts) by 4.

$$2\frac{1}{2} \div \frac{1}{4} = 2\frac{1}{2} \times 4 = 8 + 2 = 10$$

As another example, what is 10 divided by $^1/_4$? Because there are 4 fourths in each 1, and there are 10 ones in 10, there are 10 times 4 fourths in 10. So the answer is found by multiplying the dividend 10 by 4; that is, $10 \div {}^1/_4 = 10 \times 4 = 40$. To have students continue this reasoning, we can ask them to describe how to find the quotients for problems like $12 \div {}^1/_5$ and $8^1/_2 \div {}^1/_2$ and to describe in words why their solution procedures works.

Students' Reasoning and Sense Making About the Concept of Length

To further illustrate the ideas previously described, we examine students' sense making and reasoning about the concept of length. We look at the different ways that students make sense of and reason about this topic and how instruction can encourage and support students' increasingly more sophisticated reasoning about it. There are three key steps to helping students make sense of a formal mathematical idea. First, determine empirically how they currently are making sense of the idea. Second, hypothesize how their understanding of the idea might progress. Third, choose problems and representations that can potentially help them progress to more sophisticated ways of reasoning.

The Home to School problem (fig. 1.2) provides an excellent assessment of how well young students understand the concept of length. We first examine how several students made sense of this problem; then we examine the kinds of instruction each student needs.

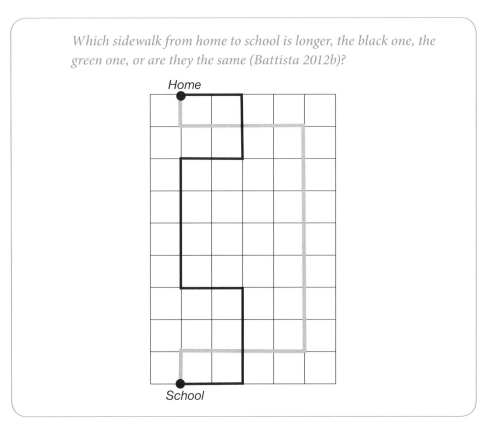

Which sidewalk from home to school is longer, the black one, the green one, or are they the same (Battista 2012b)?

Home

School

Fig. 1.2 Diagram of the two sidewalks from home to school

Investigating Students' Reasoning and Sense Making

Deanna says that the black sidewalk is longer because it is more "curvy." She made personal sense of the problem by relating it to her experience of walking paths, which tend to take longer when they have many turns (often students confound the length of a path with the time it takes to walk the path).

David uses the spread between his thumb and finger to draw a straight version of the green sidewalk, one straight component at a time (drawing on the right in fig. 1.3). He uses this same procedure to construct a straight version of the black sidewalk (drawing on the left in fig. 1.3). He then compares his drawings and says that the black sidewalk is longer. This student made personal sense of the problem by straightening the paths and comparing them directly, side by side. Note that this reasoning suggests the beginnings of a valid understanding of the concept of length, and if it were done precisely (say piece by piece on a large grid), it would be mathematically correct.

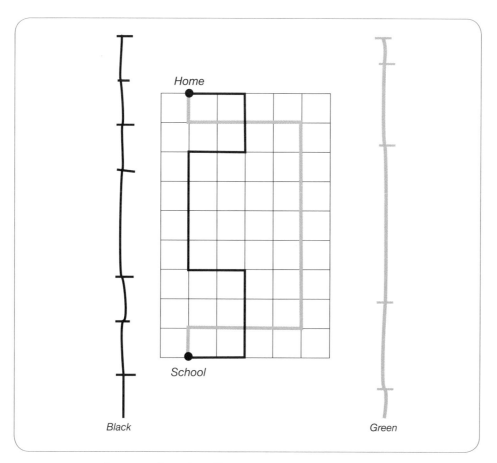

Fig. 1.3. Straightening the sidewalks

The next three students make personal sense of the problem by reasoning that they should count *something*, a strategy they have often seen used in their classrooms (see fig. 1.4). However, Molly and Matt do not yet understand exactly what to count. Molly counts whole straight sections of the sidewalks and concludes that the black sidewalk is longer. Matt has observed people counting squares along paths on similar tasks, but he does not recognize how counting squares must be done in a way that corresponds to counting unit-lengths; he concludes that the green path is longer. Only Natalie correctly counts 17 unit-lengths along each sidewalk to conclude that the two paths have the same length.

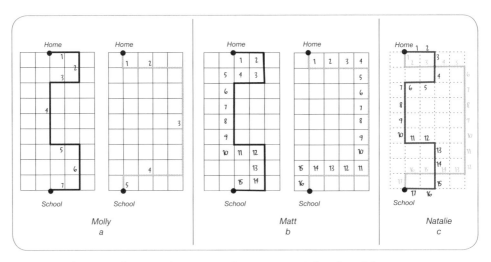

Fig. 1.4 Three students' solutions to the Home to School problem

Research Note

Difficulties in reasoning about this problem are widespread among elementary students. In individual interviews with students in grades 1–5, Battista (2012) found that there were more than twice as many students who used non-measurement strategies as those who used measurement strategies even when measurement strategies are most appropriate. Non-measurement strategies do not use numbers (like Deanna and David); measurement strategies use numbers (like Molly, Matt, and Natalie). Furthermore, no first- or second-grade students and only 6 percent of third graders, 12 percent of fourth graders, and 21 percent of fifth graders used correct measurement reasoning on this task (like Natalie). Even some adults have difficulty with this problem.

Instruction Focused on Individual Student Needs

Choosing instruction to help students like Deanna, David, Molly, and Matt make progress in understanding length measurement requires us to understand the thinking each student can build on (see Battista 2012 for a detailed description of instructional activities). For instance, we can help Deanna by having her straighten paths and compare them directly.[2] We can help David by giving him precut sticks or rods that match the straight segment lengths on the two paths, then having him make straight paths from each set of sticks to see that the paths are the same length when carefully straightened.

We can help Molly and Matt by having them physically place unit-length rods along each path, counting the unit-lengths then using the set of unit-lengths from each path to make straight versions of the paths. Because there are 17 unit-lengths in each path, when we straighten the paths, they have exactly the same length. Furthermore, most young children do not *logically* understand why counting the number of unit-lengths in the two paths tells us which is longer when straightened. They come to this conclusion *empirically* by repeatedly observing that counting predicts which path will be longer when they physically straighten the paths. It is also useful to have students compare unit-length and square iterations along grid paths to see that these iterations generally produce different counts (unless the paths are straight). Some students make sense of this discrepancy by saying that the plastic squares have to be held "sideways"— perpendicular to the student page—to give a correct count.

The key here is to help students build on what they know to make sense of increasingly more sophisticated reasoning about length. If our instruction is too abstract for students' current levels of understanding, they will not be able to make the appropriate jump in personal sense making.

Integrating Conceptual and Procedural Knowledge in Reasoning About Length

Examining the conceptual and procedural knowledge needed to solve the Home to School problem sheds additional light on student reasoning and sense making. Both types of knowledge are critical for mathematical proficiency (Kilpatrick, Swafford, and Findell 2011).

A *concept* is the meaning a person gives to things and actions. Concepts are the building blocks of reasoning: we reason by manipulating, reflecting on, and interrelating concepts that we have made sense of. *Conceptual knowledge* enables one to identify examples of and define concepts, to see relationships among concepts, and to use concepts in reasoning. For instance, we might *conceptualize* length as the linear extent of an object when it is straightened or as the distance you travel as you move along a path.

Procedural knowledge enables us to perform and use mathematical *procedures*, which are repeatable sequences of actions on objects, diagrams, or mathematical symbols. Procedural knowledge includes more than computational skill. For instance, to solve many length problems, students use the procedure of iterating and counting unit-lengths.

In the Home to School problem, Molly and Matt did not properly connect conceptual and procedural knowledge in their reasoning. These two students have not yet developed a conceptual understanding of length measurement. Molly does not understand that the iterated units must be the same length. Matt does not understand that the iterated units must be length units, not squares. Or he thinks that iterating squares is the same as iterating unit-lengths "because they are the same size." Even more confusing for students is the fact that squares can be used to properly iterate unit-lengths for straight paths and for non-straight paths *if done very carefully*. Indeed, understanding the difference between iterating squares as squares and using squares to iterate unit-lengths is extremely difficult for many students. If Matt thinks that counting squares iterates unit-lengths, he may not have sufficient conceptual understanding of unit-length iteration to guide the correct use of squares to iterate unit-lengths; that is, his iteration of squares will be correct only if the whole sidewalk path is covered by a sequence of unit-lengths, with no gaps or overlaps in the sequence.

Summary

This discussion of the Home to School problem illustrates that students often make sense of the same formal mathematical idea in different ways during the process of learning and that if instruction is to promote and support reasoning and sense making, it must be chosen to help each student build on his or her current mathematical ideas.

Observing How Instruction Can Help Students Develop the Concept of Unit-Length Iteration

We now examine how teaching can help students develop a concept of unit-length iteration that is abstract and powerful enough to deal correctly with the Home to School problem. First we look at instruction that preceded the presentation of the Home to School problem. Then we examine how the students made sense of the problem in light of the concepts about unit-length iteration they had already developed.

Six students are working together with their teacher. The students are working on a sequence of problems of increasing difficulty, starting with the following problem.

Unit-Length Problem. Which wire is longer, or are they the same length? Suppose I pull the wires so they are straight. Which would be longer? Can you check your answers with inch-rods? Can counting anything help you solve this problem?

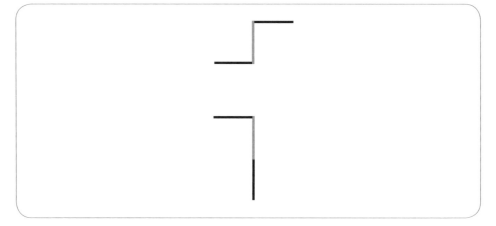

Fig. 1.5. Which wire is longer, or are they the same?

The students made sense of and reasoned about this problem in a variety of ways.

Michael: I think they might be the same length because it's curved.

Kerri: [*Uses the eraser end of her pencil to move upward on the vertical segment of the bottom wire*] 1, 2, . . . 6, [*pointing at the horizontal segment of the bottom wire*] 7. [*Uses the eraser to count the 3 unit segments on the top wire*]. 1, 2, 3; 3 plus a little more. The bottom wire is longer.

Zack: Two on this [*puts pencil horizontal then slightly vertical on the bottom wire*]. And 3 on this [*puts the pencil horizontal, vertical, then horizontal on the top wire*]. I think the top one is longer. [*Note that this is the same type of straight-section reasoning used by Molly.*]

Brandi: Wait! I would say they're the same. Like this would be [*points at the bottom black vertical segment of the bottom wire*] like this [*points at the bottom black horizontal segment of the top wire (see fig. 1.6)*]. And this line [*points at the green vertical segment of the bottom wire*] would fit here [*points on the green vertical segment of the top wire*] and this line [*points at the horizontal black segment of the bottom wire*] would fit here [*points at the top black horizontal segment of the top wire*].

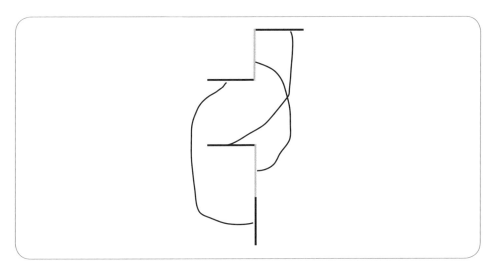

Fig. 1.6. Brandi's comparison of the unit-lengths

Gerald: I thought this one was longer [*top wire*] because I measured by using my fingers [*shows a finger spread*].

Kerri:	The line might be an inch [*pointing at the top segment of the bottom wire*]. Then I would know that it would be 3 inches on there [*goes over the bottom wire*] and maybe 3 inches on there [*goes quickly over the top wire*]. So the same.
Teacher:	Do you want to check with the inch-rods [*straws cut into 1-inch pieces*]? Each one of these is 1 inch long.
Kerri:	1, 2, 3 [*moves an inch-rod along the bottom wire*]. 1, 2, 3 [*moves an inch-rod along the top wire*]. They're the same length.
Teacher:	Without using those inch-rods, is there anything that you could use to solve this problem by counting?
Brandi:	1, 2, 3 [*pointing to segments on the bottom wire*]. 1, 2, and 3 [*pointing to segments on the top wire*].

There is a wide variety of sophistication in students' reasoning about this problem, from Michael's non-measurement reasoning, to Kerri and Zack's incorrect counting, to Brandi's non-measurement but correct one-to-one correspondence, to Kerri's correct counting. To encourage and support the students in moving toward more sophisticated reasoning, the teacher not only provides students an opportunity to check their answers but also has them reflect on how they could have solved this problem by counting unit-lengths. Note, however, that some students' sense making would have benefitted from putting 3 unit-lengths on two separate wires, counting the unit-lengths, and then actually straightening each wire. Also note how Brandi seemed to have made sense of Kerri's counting procedure and incorporated it into her own reasoning.

After several other problems, students are given the problem represented in figure 1.7.

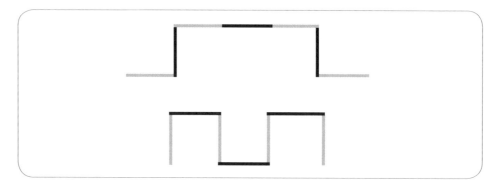

Fig. 1.7

Zack:	1, 2, 3, 4, 5, 6, 7 [*points at segments on the top wire*]. 1, 2, 3, 4, 5, 6, 7 [*points at segments on the bottom wire*]. Both are the same.
Kerri:	[*Counts 7 unit-segments on each wire*] Yep.

Serena makes a slash on each segment on both wires as she counts (fig. 1.8a), while Michael writes numbers on the segments for both wires as he counts (fig. 1.8b).

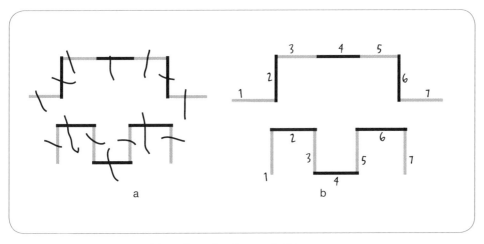

Fig. 1.8. Serena's work (a) and Michael's work (b)

Teacher:	And do you want to check them with the inch-rods?
Kerri:	Yeah.
Several students:	No.

By the end of this session, the students were routinely counting unit-lengths to compare the lengths of the wires in problems like those previously shown.

Two weeks later the teacher returned to the topic of length and had her students work on the Home to School problem (fig. 1.2), each with his or her own two activity sheets, one path per sheet. Although the students routinely used unit-length (inch) counting on the previous set of problems, in the new context of the Home to School problem, students abandoned this strategy. Because the sidewalk paths are drawn on square inch-grids, squares become visually salient for the students. Their concept of unit-length iteration was not abstract and general enough to apply in this new situation. The dialogue below illustrates how students' sense making in this new situation evolved.

Teacher:	When we're trying to figure out the lengths of the sidewalks, what should we count?
Gwen:	I think we should count the squares because they're like an inch.
Kerri:	The squares are as long as the segments. [*Points at a square along a sidewalk, then at its side*] So they're the same length, which means that if you chose either one of them it wouldn't be wrong, because they're the same length. [*Pause*] Well, you won't for sure come up with the same answer. Cause there's more squares than

segments. Oh wait! Then you could just like count the squares that are nearest [*pointing at the sidewalk*].

Gwen: And you wouldn't count ones near the corner because they're not near a segment; it's just a corner touching the line.

Kerri: You would like want to count all the ones that have a segment on them. [*Points at a segment on a sidewalk path*]

Teacher: [*Deciding that the students should all be looking at the same thing, shows Serena's sheet for the black path*] Now this part of the sidewalk you're saying is 4 blocks [*points to the squares numbered 1–4 in figure 1.9*], right?

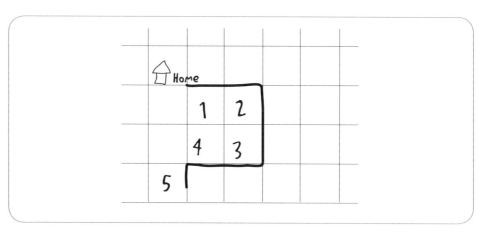

Fig. 1.9. Serena's initial count is the same as Gwen's.

Teacher: What would happen if we were measuring and we used our 1-inch straws?

Gwen: That's a problem. You can't count the squares because like they would be sharing one; this and this [*pointing at the second and third unit-segments, starting at Home*] each need a square, and we only counted one [*the 2*]. So you would need to count the sides. So we would count 1, 2, 3, 4, 5, 6, 7 around here [*correctly counting unit-lengths on the section of the sidewalk shown in figure 1.9*].

Teacher: So how long do you think the whole black sidewalk is?

Gwen: [*Correctly pointing to and counting unit-lengths along the black sidewalk*] 1, 2, . . . , 16, 17.

Teacher: 17 what?

Gwen: Sides, same as our inch straws.

Note the different ways that the students made sense of this problem during the discussion. At first, Kerri thought that using squares in the grid would work because "the squares are as long as the segments." Kerri revised her reasoning and then claimed that they should count only the squares that have a side on the sidewalk path. When Serena and Gwen seemed to do what Kerri suggested (fig. 1.9), they came up with an incorrect count. So the teacher asked a question that she thought might encourage students to revise their reasoning: "What would happen if we were measuring and we used our 1-inch straws?" After Gwen realized the difficulty with counting squares, she made sense of the correct method for iterating unit-lengths along the sidewalk paths.

This episode is an excellent example of the SMP Reason Abstractly and Quantitatively: the students had to decontextualize the unit-length counting strategy they used in the rod problems and re-contextualize it (transfer it) to apply it in the more difficult and complex context of the Home to School problem. This re-contextualizing did not occur automatically; it required reasoning and sense making above and beyond the reasoning they had applied in previous problems. In fact, it was reasoning about this new problem that led students to construct a more powerful concept of unit-length iteration that applied in more complex situations. Most often, students' initial reasoning is context dependent; it is only by giving students a variety of contexts that students decontextualize and abstract this context-dependent reasoning so that it becomes generally applicable.

Standards for Mathematical Practice and Process Standards in Sense-Making Episode

To relate our discussion of students' reasoning and sense making about the concept of length to the CCSSM Standards for Mathematical Practice (SMP) and NCTM's Process Standards (PS), we explicitly examine how the previous episodes on length are related to these practices and processes.

Standards for Mathematical Practice

Students clearly tried to make sense of the problems, but not only did the sense making differ from student to student it also evolved over instructional time. Students made sense of the concept of length by straightening paths, by matching equal sublengths, and by using increasingly more sophisticated counting (SMP 1a, b, g). They translated between different representations—numerical counting and spatial unit-iteration—both concretely and pictorially (SMP 1f). They made ever-increasing sense of counted quantities (SMP 2a). They constructed and evaluated arguments, and gave explanations and justifications for their work (SMP 3a, d, f). They applied the mathematics of counting and the concept of length to a real-world situation depicted in the Home to School problem (SMP 4a). They identified important quantities and made sense of the numerical results as their notions of what must be counted evolved (SMP 4c, d). They used appropriate tools of inch-rods (SMP 5). They attended to precision as they moved away from eraser estimations and became more precise about how counting could be used in a way relevant to the problem, in essence defining in action a definition for the appropriate unit to enumerate (SMP 6b). They communicated precisely (SMP 6a). They saw structure when they were able to use one-to-one matching of unit segments in two wires (SMP 7); that is, they saw that both wires were made from the same linear components and thus had the same length. Finally, they continually evaluated their methods (SMP 8d).

Process Standards

Clearly the students built new mathematical knowledge through problem solving by implementing, discussing, and evaluating solution strategies (PS 1a, b). They reasoned and justified, developed mathematics arguments, and communicated and evaluated their thinking and strategies (PS 2a, c; PS 3a, b). They connected counting and spatial iteration and applied mathematics (PS 4a, b). They represented spatial unit-length iteration with counting (PS 5a, b). As shown below, some students even progressed from counting to reasoning with addition and fractions (PS 4a, PS 5b).

Kerri: I separated this one in half [*draws a vertical segment separating the bottom wire into two parts (fig. 1.10)*], and I knew 4 plus 4 was 8. And the top wire is 4 plus 4 [*circling the right and left sides of the top wire*] plus 1 in the middle [*pointing*]. The top is longer.

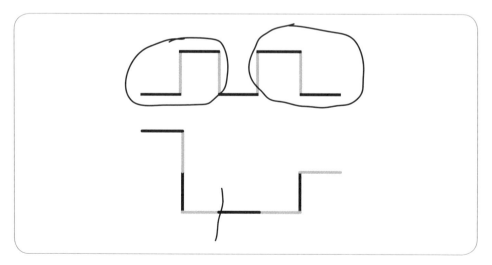

Fig. 1.10. Kerri's work

Deepening the Reasoning

The reasoning students used as described above can be extended in a number of ways. One way is to consider missing-length perimeter problems. Start with problems that help students learn to use one property of rectangles (opposite sides are equal) to find perimeter.

> *Perimeter Problem. Find the perimeter of the rectangle in figure 1.11a. (The perimeter of a shape is the distance traveled as you trace around it.) Check your answer by drawing the shape on square grid paper (see fig. 1.11b for how a student might draw the situation).*

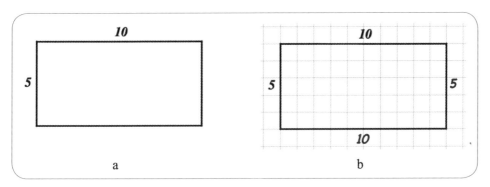

Fig. 1.11. Diagrams for the Perimeter problem

As students do several problems of this type, have them look for patterns in the measurements. They should discover that the opposite sides of rectangles are equal. Do enough problems so that students can correctly predict the perimeters before checking with grid paper (but let them check with the grids as long as they need them). After students have some proficiency with the rectangle problems, have them investigate more difficult problems such as the following.

> *Comparing Perimeters. Which shape has the greater perimeter, or do they have the same perimeter? (The perimeter of a shape is the distance traveled as you trace around it.) Finding rectangles in the shapes can help you.*

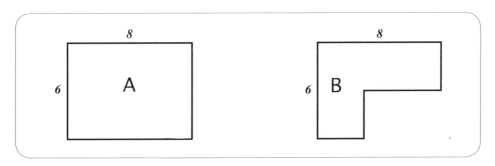

Fig. 1.12. Diagrams for Problem 3

Emily: They're the same perimeter. Because if you move this side down [*motioning along arrow* a *as shown in figure 1.13*], you get this segment [*drawing the horizontal dotted segment*]. And if you move this side over [*motioning along arrow* b], you get this segment [*drawing the vertical dotted segment*]. So the sides in B make the sides in A. They're equal.

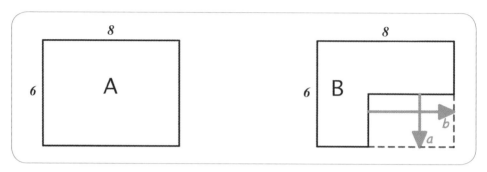

Fig. 1.13. A solution for Problem 3

Teacher: How can we check our answer?

Jordan: Maybe draw the shapes on graph paper.

Teacher: Okay, everybody do that.

Teacher: What did you find? Can somebody show us on the document projector? Jordan.

Jordan: Okay. I counted units on each side and got that A is 28 and B is 28. I also sort of checked what Emily said. See this 3 and 3 [*numbers for unknown vertical segments on the right in B in figure 1.14*] equals the 6 over here [*right vertical segment marked with 6 in A*]. And this 3 and 5 [*numbers for bottom horizontal unknown segments in B*] make 8 like the 8 down here [*bottom 8 in A*]. So Emily was right. I just needed to see the numbers to get it.

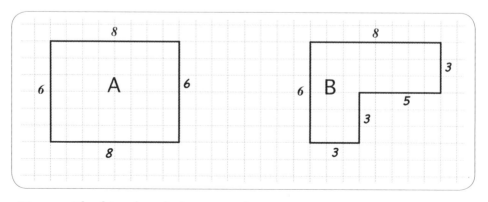

Fig. 1.14. Checking the solution on graph paper

Although some students can make sense of Emily's logical argument, many other students, like Jordan, need to see numbers to make sense of the argument. Showing both the empirical (Jordan) and logical (Emily) arguments on numerous problems will help students like Jordan start making logical arguments like Emily.

Some students will need to build shapes with interconnecting rods to help them make sense of the reasoning that if one shape can be made from the other shape by rearranging its sides, the two shapes have equal perimeters. For example, in the top portion of figure 1.15, students can use the rods to show that shape B can be made from shape A by moving rod p to the left and rod q up. For students who need more support in this sense making, we can even take the shapes apart and rearrange them in straight lines to show that they have the same length. Also, some students might reason more quantitatively that shapes A and B have the same length because they both can be made from 2 congruent long rods, 4 congruent medium rods, and 2 congruent small rods. Decomposing shapes into parts and rearranging the parts is a powerful form of geometric reasoning that is useful not only in length comparisons but also in area and volume comparisons.

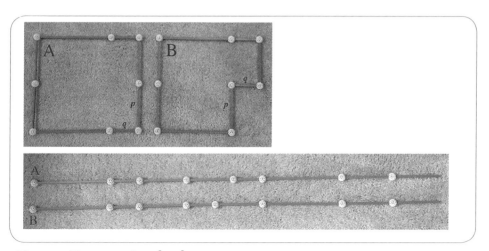

Fig. 1.15. Decomposing the shapes

Concluding Remarks on Mathematical Reasoning and Sense Making

To use mathematics to make sense of the world, students must first make sense of mathematics. To make sense of mathematics, students must transition from intuitive, informal reasoning based on their interactions with the world to precise reasoning based on formal mathematical concepts, procedures, and symbols. The key to helping students make this transition is providing appropriate instructional tasks that target precisely those concepts and ways of reasoning that students are currently ready acquire. And the key to providing this support is an understanding of research-based descriptions of the development of students' increasingly more sophisticated conceptualizations and reasoning about particular mathematical concepts. Understanding students' mathematical thinking is critical for selecting and creating instructional tasks, asking appropriate questions of students, guiding classroom discussions, adapting instruction to students' needs, understanding students' reasoning, assessing students' learning progress, and diagnosing and remediating students' learning difficulties. The chapters in this book use research on student learning to help teachers monitor, understand, and guide the development of students' reasoning and sense making about core ideas in elementary school mathematics.

Notes

1. Much of the research and development referenced in this chapter was supported in part by the National Science Foundation under Grant Numbers 0099047, 0352898, 554470, 838137, and 1119034. The opinions, findings, conclusions, and recommendations, however, are mine and do not necessarily reflect the views of the National Science Foundation.

2. For instruction on the Home to School problem, draw the paths on square-inch grid paper, and have individual inch-rods available. Also useful are sets of inch-rods strung on flexible wires so that students can make the problem paths and straighten them.

References

An, S., G. Kulm, and Z. Wu. "The Pedagogical Content Knowledge of Middle School Mathematics Teachers in China and the U.S." *Journal of Mathematics Teacher Education*, 7 (2004): 145–172.

Battista, M. T., and D. H. Clements. "Students' Understanding of Three-dimensional Rectangular Arrays of Cubes." *Journal for Research in Mathematics Education* 27, no. 3 (1996): 258–292.

Battista, M. T., D. H. Clements, J. Arnoff, K. Battista, and C. V. A. Borrow. "Students' Spatial Structuring and Enumeration of 2D Arrays of Squares." *Journal for Research in Mathematics Education*, 29, no. 5 (1998): 503–532.

Battista, M. T. "The Mathematical Miseducation of America's Youth: Ignoring Research and Scientific Study in Education." *Phi Delta Kappan* 80, no. 6 (February 1999): 424–433.

Battista, M. T. "Elementary Students' Abstraction of Conceptual and Procedural Knowledge in Reasoning about Length Measurement." Presentation given at the annual meeting of AERA, Denver, April/May 2010.

Battista, Michael T. *Cognition Based Assessment and Teaching of Geometric Measurement (Length, Area, and Volume): Building on Students' Reasoning.* Heinemann, 2012.

Borko, H., and R. T. Putnam. "Expanding a Teacher's Knowledge Base: A Cognitive Psychological Perspective on Professional Development." In *Professional Development in Education*, edited by T. R. Guskey and M. Huberman, pp. 35–65. New York: Teachers College Press, 1995.

Bransford, J. D., A. L. Brown, and R. R. Cocking. *How People Learn: Brain, Mind, Experience, and School.* Washington, D.C.: National Research Council, 1999.

Carpenter, T. P., and E. Fennema. "Research and Cognitively Guided Instruction." In *Integrating Research on Teaching and Learning Mathematics*, edited by E. Fennema, T. P. Carpenter, and S. J. Lamon, pp. 1–16. Albany: State University of New York Press, 1991.

Clarke, B., and D. Clarke. "A Framework for Growth Points as a Powerful Professional-Development Tool." Annual meeting of the American Educational Research Association, 2004.

Cobb, P., and G. Wheatley. "Children's Initial Understanding of Ten." *Focus on Learning Problems in Mathematics* 10, no. 3 (1998): 1–28.

Common Core State Standards Initiative (CCSSI). *Common Core State Standards for Mathematics.* Washington, D.C.: National Governors Association Center for Best Practices and the Council of Chief State School Officers, 2010. http://www.corestandards.org/wp-content/uploads/Math_Standards.pdf

De Corte, E., B. Greer, and L. Verschaffel. "Mathematics Teaching and Learning." In *Handbook of Educational Psychology*, edited by D. C. Berliner and R. C. Calfee, pp. 491–549. New York: Simon & Schuster/Macmillan, 1996.

Ellis, R. D. *Questioning Consciousness: The Interplay of Imagery, Cognition, and Emotion in the Human Brain.* Amsterdam/Philadelphia: John Benjamins, 1995.

Feldman, C. F., and D. A. Kalmar. "Some Educational Implications of Genre-based Mental Models: The Interpretive Cognition of Text Understanding." In *The Handbook of Education and Human Development*, edited by D. R. Olson and N. Torrance, pp. 434–460. Oxford, UK: Blackwell, 1996.

Fennema, E., and M. L. Franke. "Teachers' Knowledge and Its Impact." In *Handbook of Research on Mathematics Teaching*, edited by D. A. Grouws, pp. 127–164. Reston, Va.: National Council of Teachers of Mathematics/Macmillan, 1992.

Fennema, E., T. P. Carpenter, M. L. Franke, L. Levi, V. R. Jacobs, and S. B. Empson. "A Longitudinal Study of Learning to Use Children's Thinking in Mathematics Instruction." *Journal for Research in Mathematics Education* 27 (4): 403–434.

Greeno, J. G., A. M. Collins, and L. Resnick. "Cognition and Learning." In *Handbook of Educational Psychology*, edited by D. A. Grouws, pp. 15–46. New York: Simon & Schuster/Macmillan, 1996.

Hiebert, J., and T. P. Carpenter. "Learning and Teaching with Understanding." In *Handbook of Research on Mathematics Teaching*, D. C. Berliner, and R. C. Calfee, pp. 65–97. Reston, Va.: National Council of Teachers of Mathematics/Macmillan, 1992.

Hiebert, J., T. P. Carpenter, E. Fennema, K. C. Fuson, D. Wearne, H. Murray, A. Olivier, and P. Human. *Making Sense: Teaching and Learning Mathematics with Understanding.* Portsmouth, NH: Heinemann, 1997.

Kilpatrick, J., J. Swafford, and B. Findell. *Adding It Up: Helping Children Learn Mathematics.* Washington, D.C.: National Academy Press, 2011.

Lester, F. K. "Musing About Mathematical Problem-Solving Research: 1970–1994." *Journal for Research in Mathematics Education* 25, no. 6 (1994): 660–675.

National Council of Teachers of Mathematics (NCTM). *Principles and Standards for School Mathematics* (PSSM). Reston, Va.: NCTM, 2000.

National Research Council. *Everybody Counts.* Washington, D.C.: National Academy Press, 1989.

Prawat, R. S. "Dewey, Peirce, and the Learning Paradox." *American Educational Research Journal* 36, no. 1 (1999): 47–76.

Romberg, T. A. "Further Thoughts on the Standards: A Reaction to Apple." *Journal for Research in Mathematics Education* 23, no. 5 (1992): 432–437.

Saxe, G. B., M. Gearhart, and N. S. Nasir. "Enhancing Students' Understanding of Mathematics: A Study of Three Contrasting Approaches to Professional Support." *Journal of Mathematics Teacher Education* 4 (2001): 55–79.

Schifter, D. "Learning Mathematics for Teaching: From the Teachers' Seminar to the Classroom." *Journal for Mathematics Teacher Education* 1, no. 1 (1998): 55–87.

Schoenfeld, A. C. "What Do We Know About Mathematics Curricula." *Journal of Mathematical Behavior* 13 (1994): 55–80.

Steffe, L. P. "Schemes of Action and Operation Involving Composite Units." *Learning and Individual Differences* 4, no. 3 (1992): 259–309.

Steffe, L. P., and T. Kieren. "Radical Constructivism and Mathematics Education." *Journal for Research in Mathematics Education* 25, no. 6 (1994): 711–733.

Tirosh, D. "Enhancing Prospective Teachers' Knowledge of Children's Conceptions: The Case of Division of Fractions." *Journal for Research in Mathematics Education* 31, no. 1 (2000): 5–25.

van Hiele, P. M. *Structure and Insight.* Orlando: Academic Press, 1986.

Numerical Reasoning: Making Sense of Numbers and Operations through Multiplication in Grades 3–5

Jae Meen Baek

One of the challenging but potentially rewarding mathematical concepts that students in grades 3–5 will encounter is multiplication. In addition to its inherently rich context, multiplication can provide students with opportunities to reason about and make sense of numbers and operations. However, when it is presented as a collection of isolated facts or rules to memorize, multiplication can become tedious or confusing. For example, consider a fourth grader who was trying to solve the multiplication problem 37 × 6 by using the standard algorithm. As figure 2. 1 shows, she began skip counting by sevens six times to find the product of 7 × 6: 7, 14, 21, 28, 35, 42. She then carried the 4 tens in 42, adding it to the 3 tens in 37. Knowing that another 7 × 6 is 42, she wrote 422 as her answer. Observing many fourth and fifth graders, we see that many of them make the same error when they try to memorize steps in the traditional multiplication algorithm.

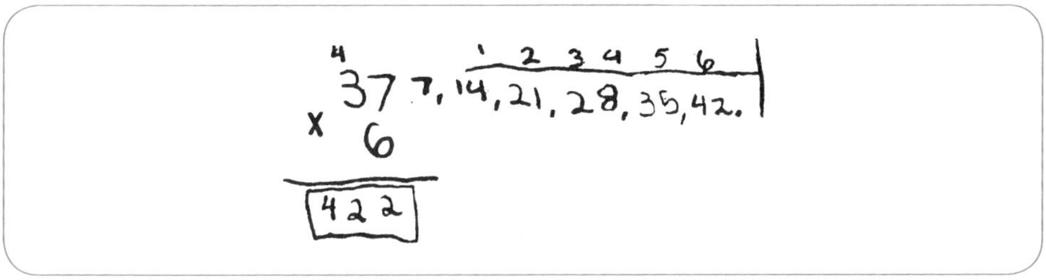

Fig. 2.1. Erroneous use of the standard algorithm for multiplication (Baek 2005)

On the other hand, a number of students solve multiplication problems by using strategies that demonstrate their proficient reasoning about numbers and multiplication. For example, when Erin, a fifth grader, was asked to figure out the total cost of 47 children who each pay $34 to go on a trip, she set up a table (fig. 2.2) and explained her strategy as follows:

Erin: It costs $34 for 1 child, so it's $340 for 10 children. Then, I wanted to figure out 50 children but did not want to add 340 five times. I knew a half of $340 would be for 5 children—that's $170. For 50 children, it would be 10 times that, and that's $1,700. But that's too much. I have to subtract the amount for 3 children to get the amount for 47 children.

Teacher: I see. How did you figure out the cost for 3 children?

Erin: I multiplied 3 times 34 in my head: 3 times 30 is 90, 3 times 4 is 12, and 90 plus 12 is 102. Then I subtracted 100 from 1,700 and subtracted 2 more. That gave me the answer, $1,598.

Task 1: There are 47 children going on a trip. If it costs $34 for each child, how much will it cost for all 47 children to go on this trip?

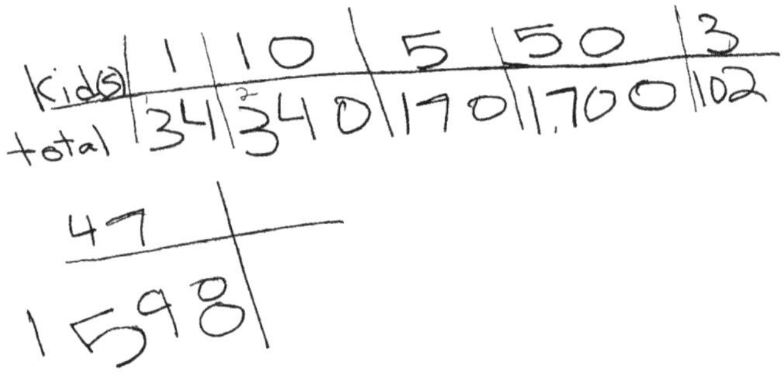

Fig. 2.2. Erin's strategy for 47 children paying $34 each (Baek 2005)

Erin's strategy exemplifies conceptually sound and meaningful student reasoning in the context of whole number multiplication. Her strategy demonstrates powerful reasoning about the meaning of multiplication as well as an understanding of the base-ten structure of the numbers. In addition, her reasoning is based on the associative and distributive properties, even though she has no explicit knowledge of these properties; that is, she has not been taught this strategy or properties in class. In this chapter, we examine student strategies like Erin's that exemplify conceptually sound reasoning and sense making in the context of multiplication word problems and discuss how instruction can support students' growth in this reasoning.

Mathematical Understanding and Common Core State Standards for Mathematics

Recently, the Common Core State Standards for Mathematics (CCSSM; NGA Center and CCSSO 2010) have articulated what mathematics students should understand and be able to do, and have emphasized the importance of numerical reasoning. More specifically, CCSSM Standards for Mathematical Practices (SMP) discuss the importance of students' ability to make sense of a problem (SMP 1) and to make sense of quantities and their relationships in a given problem situation (SMP 2). Grade-level content standards in CCSSM emphasize that quantitative reasoning entails the consistent considerations of the units involved, the meaning of quantities, and the knowledge and flexible use of properties of operations.

In the last few decades, there have been numerous publications and discussions in mathematics education communities about understanding and reasoning. For example, Carpenter and Lehrer (1999) identified several advantages of learning mathematics with understanding. First, it is easier for students to recall or reconstruct solution strategies if they understand the reasoning underlying the strategies. Second, students can extend and apply knowledge they understand. Last, students can develop ownership of their knowledge when they are given opportunities to articulate their reasoning. A longitudinal study by Carpenter and his colleagues (1998) argued that a hallmark of children's understanding is their use of invented strategies rather than formal algorithms. This study provided evidence that students who understood procedures developed a better understanding of fundamental concepts, demonstrated flexibility in transferring their knowledge to extension problems, and made significantly fewer systematic errors in their computation.

Numerical Reasoning and Common Core State Standards for Mathematics

What does it look like when students in grades 3–5 demonstrate fluent numerical reasoning? In this chapter we discuss students' numerical reasoning and the types of instruction that help develop such reasoning using student-constructed multiplication strategies observed in nine grade 3–5 classrooms as examples. In the course of this discussion, we focus on sense making of word problems, fluent strategizing based on properties of operations, and making connections between base-ten concepts and multiplying multiples of ten. These three characteristics, identified in CCSSM as evidence of students' fluency in multiplication, are so tightly connected that students who develop a proficiency in one have a solid basis for becoming proficient in another. We examine student reasoning and strategies to elaborate each characteristic and its connections.

Making Sense of Multiplication in Word Problems

Dinah, a fourth grader, used the strategy shown in figure 2.3 when she solved a problem about the total number of M&Ms in 23 bags with 177 M&Ms per bag. She explained her strategy as follows.

Dinah: I first added 2 bags: that's 354 M&Ms. Then I doubled that: that's 4 bags and 708 M&Ms. I kept on doing that. When I got to 16 bags, I knew it would be too much if I doubled that, so I added 8 bags. That's 24 bags and 4,248 M&Ms. Then I knew the problem was about 23 bags, so I subtracted 177 from 4,248: that's 4,071. That's my answer.

Teacher: [*While pointing at the circled numbers on the left*] Why did you circle these numbers?

Dinah: I wanted to keep track of bags.

Dinah's strategy shows she clearly understood that in this problem, 23 represented the number of bags and 177 represented the number of M&Ms in each bag. She devised a notation that distinguished the number of bags from the number of M&Ms by circling the number of bags, which appears to have aided her in adjusting her solution from the number of M&Ms in 24 bags to the number in 23 bags.

Task 2: Mrs. Parker had 23 bags of M&Ms for Halloween. Each bag contained 177 M&Ms. How many M&Ms did Mrs. P have?

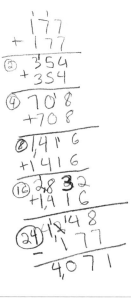

Fig. 2.3. Dinah's strategy for 23 bags of 177 M&Ms per bag

In contrast, when students are not clear about what each factor in a multiplication problem represents, they can get confused what to do with those factors. Consider the two strategies employed by Debbie and Tom in figure 2.4. Both students were solving a problem about the total number of children in 24 classes with 32 children per class. The following are their explanations.

Debbie: First, I added ten 32s because that would give me the answer for 10 classes. I did 320 plus 320 equals 640; that's 20 classes. Then I added 4 to 640.

Teacher: Can you explain why you added 4 to 640?

Debbie: Because 640 is for 20. The problem is about 24, not 20.

Tom: I multiplied 20 times 30; that's 600. 4 times 2 is the same as 4 plus 4; that's 8. 600 plus 8 is 608.

Teacher: Can you explain why you did 20 times 30 and 4 times 2?

Tom: Because 24 is 20 and 4, and 30 is 30 and 2.

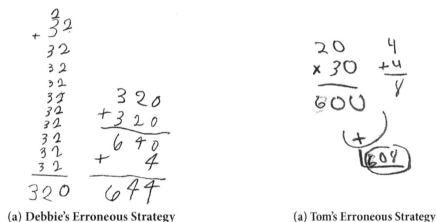

Task 3: An elementary school has 24 classes. If there are 32 children in each class, how many children are there at the school?

(a) Debbie's Erroneous Strategy   (a) Tom's Erroneous Strategy

Fig. 2.4. Two erroneous strategies for the problem of 24 classes with 32 children in each class

The errors in these two strategies are different but share a common struggle with what the factors 24 and 32 mean in the given problem. This task can be challenging, especially when factors in a problem are large and students choose to partition large factors into smaller numbers, in the process of which they sometimes lose track of what each of the factors means. In this example, Debbie understood that 20 from 24 represents 20 classes, but she forgot that 4 represents 4 classes, not 4 children. Because of this error, in her last step of adding 640 and 4, Debbie added 640 children (in 20 classes) to 4 classes instead of adding 640 children (in 20 classes) to the number of children in 4 classes. In Tom's strategy, after decomposing 24 into 20 and 4 and 32 into 30 and 2, he failed to keep track of the facts that 20 and 4 represent the number of classes and that 30 and 2 represent the number of children in each class. If he had kept track, Tom would have realized that the sum of 20×30 and 4×2 computes 20 classes with 30 children in each class and 4 classes with 2 children in each class, which means that none of the 24 classes in his computation had 32 children.

It is not uncommon to observe errors similar to Debbie's and Tom's even in higher-level mathematics classes. For example, many middle or high school students make an error in using the distributive property for expressions such as $x(4x + y)$ or $(x + y)(2x + 3y)$ and incorrectly think $x(4x + y)$ is equivalent to $4x^2 + y$ or $(x + y)(2x + 3y)$ is equivalent to $2x^2 + 3y^2$. If teachers can consistently support students in clarifying the meaning of each factor and what it means to express a factor as a sum of two numbers, they will help students avoid making errors like those in the example. Elementary teachers can start the effort by encouraging students to discuss each factor and partial product by using the references in the given problem, so that students can reason what each of the partial products in their computation represents and whether it makes sense to add certain quantities. It is interesting to note that both Erin (fig. 2.2) and Dinah (fig. 2.3) utilized representations to help them keep track of different references of two factors. Erin clearly labeled the top row as "kid(s)" and the bottom row as "total," while Dinah circled the number of classes to visually distinguish them from the number of children.

Some students used more subtle notations to keep track of the factors. Their explanations, however, revealed that they had developed a systematic way of doing so. For example, Sean, a fourth grader, used the strategy shown in figure 2.5 to solve a problem about 153 bags with 37 balloons in each bag. He decomposed each factor based on place value, such as hundreds, tens, and ones. Then he figured out each partial product and added them up for his final answer. When he was asked to explain, he responded as follows.

Sean: [*While circling the first three partial products in figure 2.5*] That's 30 balloons in 153 bags. [*While circling the last three partial products in figure 2.5*] That's 7 balloons in 153 bags.

Teacher: Why did you separate 37 balloons into 30 balloons and 7 balloons?

Sean: The numbers are too large. It is easier for me if I count 30 balloons in 153 bags first and the rest second.

It is clear that Sean mentally kept track of what each partial product represented and could reason through why the sum of the six partial products represents the total number of balloons.

Task 4: Mr. Party has 153 bags of balloons at his party product store. Each bag has 37 balloons. How many balloons does Mr. Party have at his store?

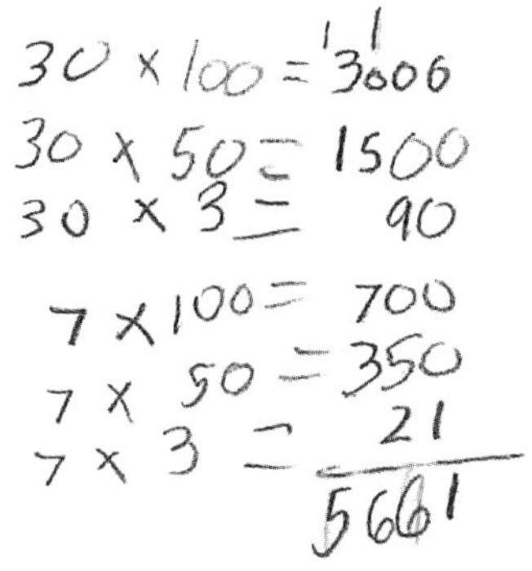

$$30 \times 100 = 3006$$
$$30 \times 50 = 1500$$
$$30 \times 3 = 90$$
$$7 \times 100 = 700$$
$$7 \times 50 = 350$$
$$7 \times 3 = 21$$
$$5661$$

Fig. 2.5. Sean's strategy for 153 bags with 37 balloons in each bag

Student Strategies Based on Properties of Operations

Students' understanding of what factors represent in a multiplication problem appears to assist them in constructing strategies that are based on properties of operations, which is highly emphasized as one of the important aspects of number concepts and operations. The Common Core Standards lists $8 \times 7 = 8 \times (5 + 2) = (8 \times 5) + (8 \times 2)$ and $(3 \times 5) \times 2 = 3 \times (5 \times 2)$ as examples of strategies based on the distributive and associative properties of multiplication (NGA Center and CCSSO 2010, p. 23). We know, based on classroom observation, that a large percentage of the grade 3–5 students who understand the meaning of multiplication word problems construct strategies based on properties of operations similar to those in the examples in CCSSM. For example, in solving the problem about 7 bags of candy with 34 pieces of candy in each bag, Aaron, a fourth grader, decomposed 34 into 30 and 4. Then he solved 7×34 as the sum of 7×30 and 7×4, which is based on the distributive property of multiplication over addition (fig. 2.6).

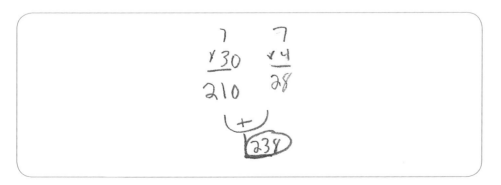

Fig. 2.6. Aaron's strategy for 7 bags of 34 pieces of candy in each bag

When problems involve multidigit numbers for both factors, some children partition *both* factors and generate multiple partial products. Sean's strategy in fig. 2.5 is a good example of such partitioning. The following symbolic representation of Sean's strategy explicitly displays the distributive property embedded in his strategy:

$$37 \times 153 = (30 + 7) \times (100 + 50 + 3)$$
$$= (30 \times 100) + (30 \times 50) + (30 \times 3)) + (7 \times 100) + (7 \times 50) + (7 \times 3)$$

Interestingly, more students partition only one of the two factors, instead of partitioning both factors, when both factors are multidigit numbers. For example, Laura, a fifth grader, solved a problem about the total number of balloons in 153 bags with 37 balloons in each bag by partitioning 153 into 100, 50, and 3 but did not partition 37 (Baek 2005). Here is how Laura explained her strategy (fig. 2.7):

Teacher: Can you explain how you solved this problem?

Laura: I know 100 times 37 is 3,700. 50 is a half of 100, so I need a half of 3,700. A half of 700 is 350, and a half of 3,000 is 1,500. 350 plus 1,500 is 1,850. I added three 37s for 3 more bags. I added them all, and got 5,661.

Task 5: Mr. Party has 153 bags of balloons at his party product store. Each bag has 37 balloons. How many balloons does Mr. Party have at his store?

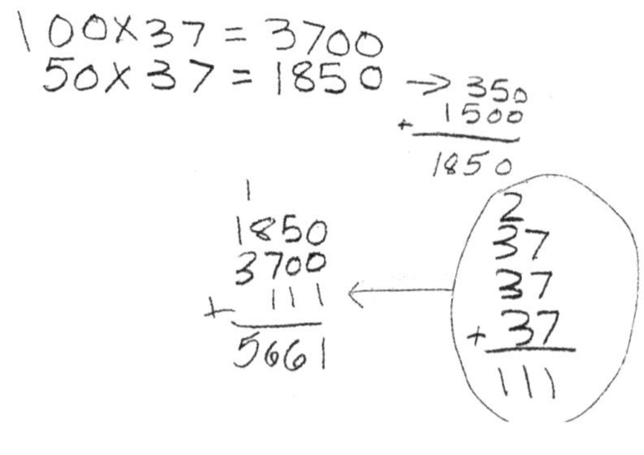

Fig. 2.7. Laura's strategy for 153 bags of 37 balloons

The following symbolic representation of Laura's strategy explicitly displays the distributive and associative properties of multiplication embedded in her strategy.

$$
\begin{aligned}
153 \times 37 &= (100 + 50 + 3) \times 37 \\
&= (100 \times 37) + (50 \times 37) + (3 \times 37) && \text{[Distributive Property]} \\
&= (100 \times 37) + [(\tfrac{1}{2} \times 100) \times 37)] + (3 \times 37) \\
&= (100 \times 37) + \tfrac{1}{2} \times (100 \times 37) + (3 \times 37) && \text{[Associative Property of Multiplication]} \\
&= (100 \times 37) + \tfrac{1}{2} \times [100 \times (30 + 7)] + (3 \times 37) \\
&= (100 \times 37) + \tfrac{1}{2} \times [(100 \times 30) + (100 \times 7)] + (3 \times 37) \\
&= (100 \times 37) + [\tfrac{1}{2} \times (100 \times 30) + \tfrac{1}{2} \times (100 \times 7)] + (3 \times 37) && \text{[Distributive Property]}
\end{aligned}
$$

Laura's strategy in deriving 50 × 37 from 100 × 37 indicates great flexibility in her reasoning. When students construct strategies based on properties without having had direct instruction from a teacher, their strategies are often more flexible and more efficient than those based on traditionally taught algorithms.

The wide range of different strategies that students construct, however, can be a big challenge for teachers to manage in the classroom. For example, Dean used the strategy shown for the problem of 47 children costing $34 each. After completing the strategy shown in figure 2.8, Dean explained his reasoning as follows.

Dean: First, I did 10 times 30, which is 300. I added 300 four times; that's 40 times 30. Then I did 7 times 30: that's 210. So far, I did 47 children paying $30. Then I did 47 times 4: that's 188.

Teacher: How did you figure out 47 times 4?

Dean: I knew 47 times 2 is 94, so I doubled it in my head and got 188.

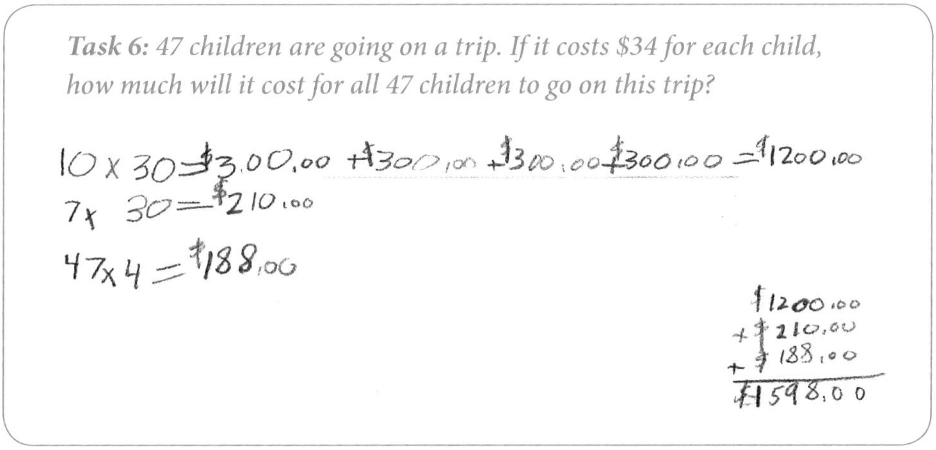

Task 6: 47 children are going on a trip. If it costs $34 for each child, how much will it cost for all 47 children to go on this trip?
10 x 30=$300.00 +$300.00 +$300.00 $300.00 =$1200.00
7x 30=$210.00
47x4 =$188.00
$1200.00
+$210.00
+$188.00
$1598.00

Fig. 2.8. Dean's strategy for 47 children paying $34 each

Although he incorrectly used the equals sign in the equation 10 × 30 = 300 + 300 + 300 + 300 = 1,200,[1] Dean's strategy shows a flexibility that we usually do not see in the strategies of students who are taught a multiplication algorithm to follow. Also it is based on both the distributive and associative properties. Dean partitioned $34 into 30 and 4. In multiplying $30 by 47, he partitioned 47 into 40 and 7, and computed 40×30 and 7×30. In computing 40×30, Dean went further, partitioning 40 into 4 groups of 10, and then, recalling his use of 10×30, he added the partial product four times to figure out 40×30. In computing 47×4, instead of computing 40×7 and 4×4, Dean doubled 47 and doubled 94 again. His strategy can be represented as the following in order to display underlying properties more explicitly:

$$
\begin{aligned}
47 \times 34 &= 47 \times (30 + 4) \\
&= (47 \times 30) + (47 \times 4) && \text{[Distributive Property]} \\
&= (40 + 7) \times 30 + (47 \times 4) \\
&= [(40 \times 30) + (7 \times 30)] + (47 \times 4) && \text{[Distributive Property]} \\
&= \{[(4 \times 10) \times 30] + (7 \times 30)\} + (47 \times 4) \\
&= \{[4 \times (10 \times 30)] + (7 \times 30)\} + (47 \times 4) && \text{[Associative Property]} \\
&= \{[4 \times (10 \times 30)] + (7 \times 30)\} + [47 \times (2 \times 2)] \\
&= \{[4 \times (10 \times 30)] + (7 \times 30)\} + [(47 \times 2) \times 2] && \text{[Associative Property]}
\end{aligned}
$$

Base-Ten Concepts and Multiplication

The Common Core Standards emphasizes multiplication strategies based on base-ten concepts, starting with a single-digit number times multiples of ten in grade 3 and going all the way to multiplying a number by any power of ten in grade 5. Although the standards do not provide examples of what multiplication strategies based on base-ten concepts look like, there are several concepts that mathematics education research has identified as being key to students' understanding of the base-ten structure of our number system. One of these is that a multidigit number is the sum of place-value units. For example, students are considered to have a grasp of the basic structure of the base-ten system when they understand 64 as the sum of 6 groups of tens and 4 groups of ones without having to model and count (Carpenter et al. 2015). Another is that the value of each place from right to left increases by ten times.

Many students in grades 4 and 5 use knowledge of base-ten concepts in multiplying multidigit numbers. Aaron's strategy in figure 2.6 is a good example of this. In solving the problem of 7 groups of 34, he knew that $34 = 30 + 4$ and computed 7×30 and 7×4. However, a small number of students who identified the number of tens and ones in a two-digit number did not take advantage of that knowledge when they solved multidigit multiplication problems. For example, in solving a problem about finding the total number of blocks in 35 sets with 23 blocks in each set, Bob, a fourth grader, thought of 35 as 7 groups of 5. As shown in figure 2.9, he computed 5 sets of 23 and repeatedly added this partial product seven times to reach the answer (Baek 2005). Although this strategy demonstrated fluent understanding of the problem and was based on the distributive property, it did not take full advantage of the base-ten structure of 35 as 3 groups of tens and 5 groups of ones.

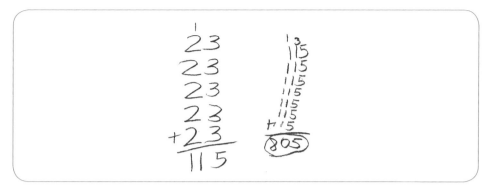

Fig. 2.9. Bob's strategy for 35 sets of 23 blocks in each set

Some students partitioned one of the factors based on the base-ten structure but did not know the product for a number times ten as a number fact. When they did not know those number facts, their strategies for large-number multiplication were often long and tedious. For example, Michelle solved the problem of 153 bags of 37 balloons per bag by starting to add 37 ten times to figure out the number of balloons in 10 bags (fig. 2.10). Then she added 370 ten times to figure out 100 bags. She added 370 fives times for 50 bags and 37 three times for 3 more bags. Finally she added all the partial products to answer the problem. We will see how knowledge of multiplying by multiples of ten can be used in this problem in our discussion of Kate's reasoning on the same problem.

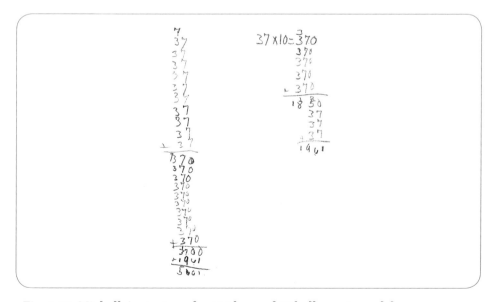

Fig. 2.10. Michelle's strategy for 153 bags of 37 balloons in each bag

In solving the same problem about the number of balloons, Kate, a fifth grader, partitioned 153 bags using her place-value understanding like Michelle did. The difference was that Kate knew the product of 10 × 37 and 100 × 37 as recalled number facts. After completing the strategy illustrated in figure 2.11, Kate explained her reasoning as follows.

Kate: I knew 10 times 37 is 370, so I added 370 five times for 50 bags: that's 1,850. I added 3,700 to 1,850, because 37 times 100 is 3,700: that's 150 bags. Then I added three 37s.

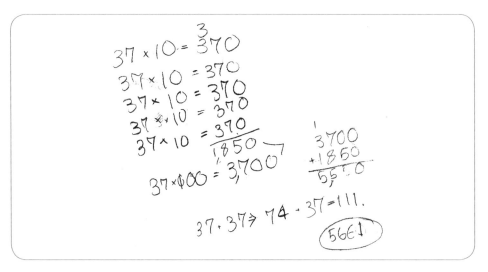

Fig. 2.11. Kate's strategy for 153 bags of 37 balloons in each bag

Both Michelle and Kate's strategies are based on understanding that 153 is the sum of 100, 50, and 3. Michelle's strategy also shows that she knew 100 is 10 groups of 10. However, since Kate knew 10 groups of 37 as a number fact, her strategy was more efficient than Michelle's. Although it is not clear if Kate's knowledge of 37 × 10 = 370 was based on an understanding of the base-ten structure of our number system or on a memorized number fact, having the knowledge of "times ten" and "times a hundred" is an important element in developing efficient strategies for multidigit whole number multiplication.

The strategies discussed thus far provide a picture of what student-generated strategies can look like when students make sense of the meaning of multiplication and know the properties of numbers and the base-ten structure of our number system. As the examples of student reasoning and sense making have illustrated, when students developed the meaning of the multiplication operation in familiar contexts, their strategies became more fluent and often based on the distributive or associative properties, all without the benefit of direct instruction. Most students were able to create and keep track of partial products and to develop mathematical representation that supported their thinking. As shown in figure 2.4, when they did not keep track of the meaning of each partial product, the students ended up with invalid strategies. In addition, their strategies became significantly more efficient and accurate for multidigit factor problems when they utilized the base-ten structure of our number system and had number fact knowledge of multiples of ten. In summary, the student strategies we have observed demonstrate that students must understand the meaning of multiplication as well as base-ten structure if they are to become proficient in developing strategies based on the properties of multiplication as emphasized in the Common Core Standards.

Promoting Numerical Reasoning in the Classroom

Teacher instruction is critical to the development of students' numerical reasoning skills. In this section, we will discuss three key instructional strategies that specifically target the topic of whole number multiplication: (1) provide equal-grouping problems as contexts for multiplication, (2) facilitate students' construction and articulation of strategies that make sense to them, and (3) encourage students to represent their strategies mathematically.

Real-life problems provide students with a foundation for constructing meaningful strategies. The Common Core recommends equal grouping as one of the initial contexts for multiplication. Most students in grades 3–5 are familiar with equal-grouping situations, and textbooks often use them as introductory activities for learning multiplication. Consistent with the recommendations of the Common Core, however, our approach to using real-life problems is different from that used in many textbooks, which often introduce multiplication using equal-grouping stories, show repeated addition as a way to compute, and then move on to memorizing facts. In that approach, students do not work on the story problems to develop deep understanding of the operation and are instructed to move on to symbolic problems too soon. That is different from how we have seen in this chapter how contextual problems can provide a fundamental base for numerical sense making, reasoning, and problem solving.

Students' knowledge of equal-grouping situations from everyday experiences helps them construct strategies that make sense to them without teachers having to show them how to solve the problems. Constructing strategies for the problems on their own in turn helps students develop deeper understanding of the multiplicative structure (SMP 7) of those problems. Without the contextualized problems, it is more difficult for students in grades 3 or 4 to construct strategies based on distributive or associative properties. As noted in the discussion of Erin's and Dinah's strategies (figs. 2.2 and 2.3, respectively), the meaning of each factor in the equal-grouping problems often aids students in keeping track of partial products, which helps them generate strategies consistent with the distributive or associative properties without their having had any direct instruction. This approach illustrates how situated problems provide an important foundation for sense making in multiplication, not only for students who are at the beginning level of understanding the meaning of multiplication but also for those who have developed sophisticated conceptual understanding and strategies for multiplication problems. It indicates that it is helpful for students to continuously work on word problems in addition to problems in equation format.

The Common Core is emphatic in its recommendation that students in grades 2–4 learn to use multiplication strategies based on the meaning of the operation, properties of multiplication, and base-ten structure, and that the traditional multiplication algorithm be a part of standards in grade 5. These recommendations appear to be consistent with those found in the research studies by Carpenter et al. (1998) and Schwartz et al. (2011), which suggest that it is important that students invent their own strategies *before* they learn prescribed procedures. Students who attempt to use the multiplication algorithm before they construct their own strategies often have difficulty in making sense of what the algorithm is about and make errors like those we discussed in figure 2.1.

Many students in grades 3 and 4 initially use strategies that represent each and every group, which can be long, tedious, and often error prone if one or both factors in the problem are multidigit numbers. Teachers can help their students develop more efficient strategies by engaging them in class discussion. By closely monitoring the strategies of their students, teachers can support them by encouraging them to discuss what each partial product represents, to share different types of strategies, and to explain why each strategy worked in whole-class discussion. With such support, students will be more eager to discuss the differences and similarities among their strategies and to test out the strategies of other students. Such discussions can expand their understanding of various strategies, help them reflect on what they already know, and encourage them to find and use more efficient strategies. For example, we have observed teachers who implement this approach by routinely asking students to discuss the similarities and differences between strategies like those in figures 2.10 and 2.11 in the following manner.

Teacher: How are Michelle's and Kate's strategies similar to or different from each other?

Abby: They both figured out how many balloons are in 10 bags.

Matt: Michelle added 37 ten times, but Kate knew 10 times 37 is 370 right away. Kate's strategy is faster.

Emma: Kate knew 10 times 370 is 3,700. That helped her strategy be more efficient too.

Teacher:	Do we know a number times 10?
Steve:	Yes, you just add 0.
Teacher:	Do we add 0? If it is 10 times 37, do we do 37 plus 0? [*As she writes 37 + 0 = ____ on the board*] What is 37 plus 0?
Steve:	No, not adding 0. I mean, write 0 after 37.
Teacher:	[*As she writes 37_0_*] Like this?
Students:	Yes!
Teacher:	Does it work all the time? Why?
Kate:	It's because 10 times 37 is 10 times 30 and 10 times 7.
Michelle:	I think it works all the time, but I am not sure why.
Teacher:	I think we should keep on investigating this. If we know the number facts about a number times 10 or 100, do you think it will help your strategies be more efficient?
Students:	Yeah.

We have observed that many teachers urge students to discuss specific strategies such as knowing 10 × 37, so that students can determine if what they know can be generally applied to other problems involving whole numbers times ten. By participating in this type of discussion, students are often more likely to engage in metacognitive activities such as thinking about any relevant number facts they already might know, finding ways to use these facts, looking ahead at their plans to see if their strategy will work for a given problem, and determining a reasonable range for the answer before they start computational procedures.

Teachers also can help students to improve their numerical reasoning by assisting them in representing their strategies. For the students who lost track of the partial products using the strategies shown in figure 2.4, teachers can suggest that they clearly notate what each partial product represents in a way that makes sense to them. Some children labeled each row of a table like that shown in figure 2.2, and others were encouraged to add a label to their representation. For example, when Linda, a fourth grader, solved the problem of 47 children paying $34 each, she recorded what each partial product represents when her teacher asked what the first 136 represent, which helped her reason through her multiple-step strategy (fig. 2.12).

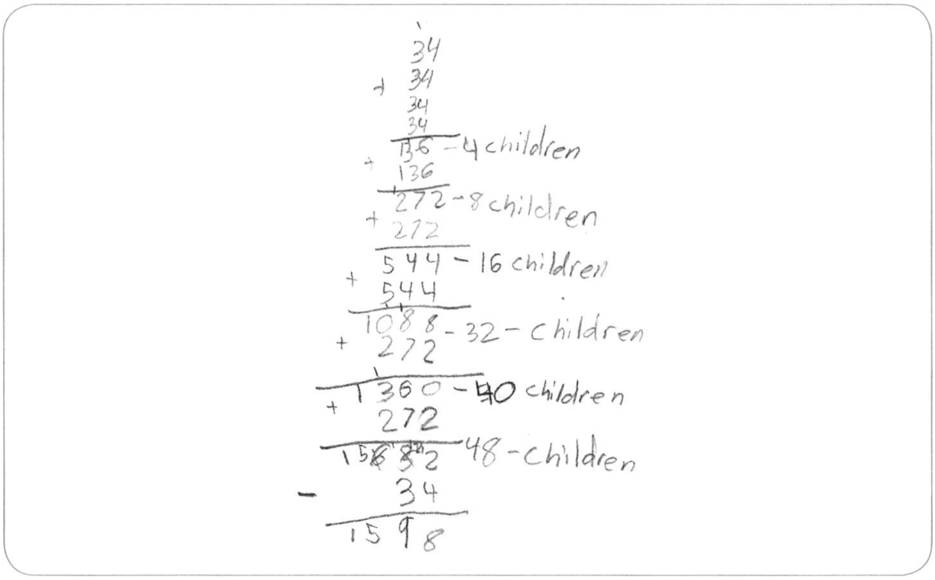

Fig. 2.12. Linda's strategy for 47 children paying $34 each

When students construct their own strategies, teachers can model how to write an equation for their strategies in a way that will provide an opportunity to explicitly discuss the distributive or associative property embedded in their strategies. Tracy's writing in figure 2.13 for the problem of 24 classes with 32 children per class is a good example of this type of opportunity. After Tracy had written out her computation on the blackboard as shown in figure 2.13, her teacher asked her to describe what she did. Tracy answered:

Tracy: I did 32×10 to figure out the number of children in 10 classes. Then I added two groups of 320 to figure out 20 classes. Then I added four 32s on the side to figure out 4 classes. I added 128 to 640 to answer the problem.

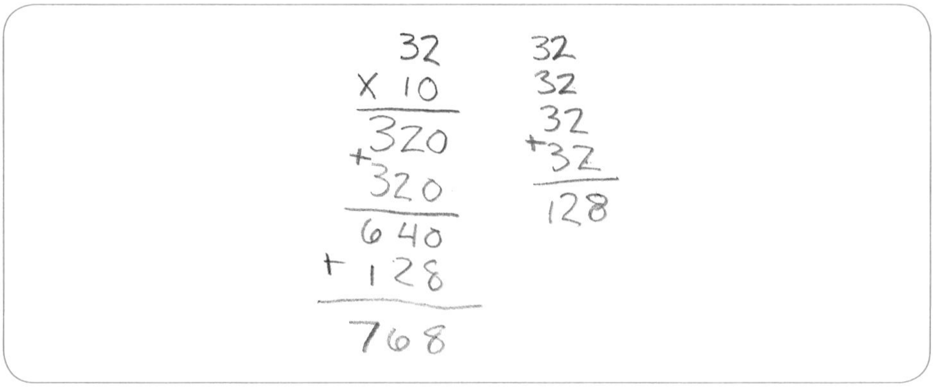

Fig. 2.13. Tracy's strategy for 24 classes with 32 children per class

Teachers can engage students by asking questions such as "Why did Tracy compute 10 groups of 32," so that students can discuss the fact that Tracy did not know the product of 24 groups of 32 right away but did know 10 groups of 32. As teachers add equations like the ones shown in the box in figure 2.14 to Tracy's strategy, they can ask follow-up questions, such as why the sum of 320, 320 and 128 is the product of 24 groups of 32, and how they know they do not need to add another 320 or 128. Such questions provide an opportunity for students to discuss how the sum of the partial products 10 × 32, 10 × 32, and 4 × 32 equals 24 × 32 because 10 + 10 + 4 = 24.

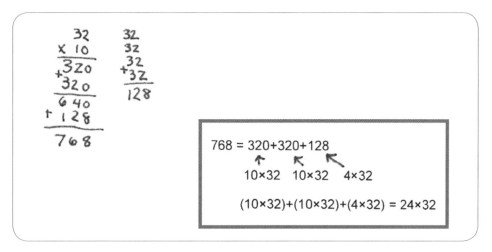

Fig. 2.14. Possible teacher's equations for Tracy's strategy

Using equations like those shown in figure 2.14 often leads to a discussion about whether or not the distributive property always works in multiplication. For example, teachers can ask students if they can find a smaller number of groups in multiple steps, such as 10 groups, 10 groups, and 4 groups, instead of 24 groups at once, no matter how many are in each group. They can ask questions to help students generalize this idea, such as "Are there are other ways to compute 24 groups by partitioning 24 differently?" "How would you partition if the total number of groups given were 42 instead of 24?" and so on. When students become proficient, they will have more opportunities to further generalize their understanding of the distributive property in a more algebraic way. Students can also work on equation problems with missing values, such as 42 × 32 = 12 × 32 + □ × 32, which is read as "42 groups of 32 is the same as 12 groups of 32 plus so many groups of 32. How many groups of 32 do you need to add to 12 groups of 32 so that it will be the same as 42 groups of 32?" Although algebraic equations are beyond the scope of this chapter, helping students write equations in a way that represents their strategies will lay an important foundation for more rigorous mathematical learning in later grades. It will support students who are trying to make sense of the distributive property rather than memorizing it as a rule.

Challenges and Conclusions

Making sense of the meaning of multiplication by using contexts and by constructing their own strategies supports students to achieve the level of fluency described in *CCSSM* (National Governors Association 2010). Although teaching multiplication as repeated addition and having students memorize multiplication facts or the formal algorithm can help computation, it is more difficult to use that line of instruction to facilitate students' construction of flexible strategies based on properties of multiplication and base-ten structure. On the contrary, the student strategies shared in this chapter demonstrate that students can and do construct proficient strategies when they are given opportunities to make sense of multiplication in a context with which they are familiar and encouraged to construct and discuss their own strategies.

In this chapter, we have discussed several strategies at different levels of mathematical sophistication by focusing on the properties of multiplication and base-ten concepts. We discussed instructional strategies that can help students develop proficient strategies in the classroom. We also reflected on how this type of instruction presents teachers with several challenges and why these challenges necessitate more professional development support for teachers. Although classroom teachers face many challenges, there are three that stand out. First, teachers need to familiarize themselves with the strategies that students often construct, which can range from concrete to very sophisticated. Although such strategizing is a sign of understanding, the impressively wide range of students' strategies and representations makes it difficult for teachers to distinguish which are different mathematically and developmentally, and which are mathematically the same but represented differently.

Second, it is difficult to recognize properties of multiplication when they are embedded in students' strategies. In work with pre- and in-service teachers, we often discuss, for example, a student-constructed strategy like Tracy's in figure 2.13 and ask if it is based on a property or not. If it is, teachers should name the property and explain how they reached their conclusion. Many teachers initially have difficulty identifying the distributive property embedded in Tracy's strategy although they can identify an equation representing the distributive property when it is represented in a more typical algebraic equation, such as $s \times (t + p) = s \times t + s \times p$.

Third, teachers must learn as much as they can about students' thinking and mathematics and be able to orchestrate discussions that help students use equations to represent their strategies. Representing strategies using equations can help students understand the relationships of the numbers and operations they have reasoned through. Equations can also become a tool for examining the basis of mathematical relationships more explicitly, thereby providing students with opportunities to advance their learning as far as algebra. It is, however, a challenging task to write equations that represent students' strategies in a way that students can see their thinking *in them*. For example, what if a teacher had written the equation $(20 \times 32) + (4 \times 32) = 24 \times 32$ for Tracy's strategy in figure 2.13 instead of $(10 \times 32) + (10 \times 32) + (4 \times 32)$? Although the equation $(20 \times 32) + (4 \times 32) = 24 \times 32$ is not incorrect, Tracy or other students may not see it as a representation of her thinking; they may see $(20 \times 32) + (4 \times 32)$ as a different strategy. In addition, discussing how to represent strategies using equations is more productive when timing is appropriate. Many teachers have found that students are more successful at writing equations when they are fluently using and discussing strategies that are based on one of the properties of multiplication. This means that teachers need to know about the types of strategies that students use and their level of fluency as well as mathematics.

The challenges discussed in this section are only a few of the many that teachers face when they focus on promoting sense making and reasoning in mathematics in grades 3–5. They each may differ slightly from one another in how they need to be met, but they are all connected to knowing students' thinking and related mathematical contents. That said, teachers should not wait to teach for reasoning until they are totally familiar with students' thinking and master mathematical contents. A critical starting point of this journey is to provide students with word problems and encourage them to construct strategies that make sense to them and whose efficacy they can explain. The student strategies and representations described in this chapter demonstrate that students can develop numerical reasoning at a high level when they are provided with these opportunities. Not only can students understand the meaning of operations, but they can also construct strategies they can explain. Surprisingly these strategies can reach a level of mathematical sophistication that is based on mathematical properties and our base-ten number system as stated in the Common Core. Learning about student thinking and mathematical content takes time and patience. However, teachers can start by providing appropriate tasks and cultivating an environment that encourages discussion so that more students in grades 3–5 develop mathematical reasoning skills in arithmetic and develop a foundational understanding for algebra in later grades, while teachers learn about student strategies along with their students.

Note

1. Dean's use of the equals sign is incorrect because 10×30 is not equal to the sum of $300 + 300 + 300 + 300$. A correct use of equals sign would have been $10 \times 30 = 300$; $300 + 300 + 300 + 300 = 1,200$.

References

Baek, Jae Meen. "Children's Mathematical Understanding and Invented Strategies for Multidigit Multiplication," *Teaching Children Mathematics* 12 (2005/2006): 242–247.

Carpenter, Thomas P. and Richard Lehrer. "Teaching and Learning Mathematics with Understanding." In *Mathematics Classrooms that Promote Understanding*, edited by Elizabeth Fennema and Thomas A. Romberg, pp. 19–32. Mahwah, NJ: Erlbaum, 1999.

Carpenter, Thomas P., Elizabeth Fennema, Megan L. Franke, Linda Levi, and Susan B. Empson. *Children's Mathematics: Cognitively Guided Instruction, Second Edition.* Portsmouth, NH: Heinemann, 2015.

Carpenter, Thomas P., Megan L. Franke, Victoria R. Jacobs, Elizabeth Fennema, and Susan B. Empson. "A Longitudinal Study of Invention and Understanding in Children's Multidigit Addition and Subtraction," *Journal for Research in Mathematics Education* 29 (1998): 3–20.

National Governors Association Center for Best Practices (NGA Center) and Council of Chief State School Officers (CCSSO). *Common Core State Standards for Mathematics. Common Core State Standards (College- and Career-Readiness Standards and K–12 Standards in English Language Arts and Math).* Washington, D.C.: NGA Center and CCSSO, 2010. http://www.corestandards.org

Schwartz, Daniel L., Catherine C. Chase, Marily A. Oppezzo, and Doris B. Chin, "Practicing Versus Inventing With Contrasting Cases: The Effects of Telling First on Learning and Transfer," *Journal of Educational Psychology* 103 (2011): 757–775.

Numerical Reasoning: Number and Operations with Fractions

3

Kathleen Cramer

Helping students to broaden their understanding of number to include fractions is an important instructional goal for teachers of students in grades 3–5. Students can build number sense for fractions and learn to reason with fractions by using different representations, including concrete models, pictures, and story contexts involving equal-sharing situations.

Key elements of reasoning and sense making with fractions includes the following:

- *Judging the relative size of fractions.* Based on mental representations connected to their experiences with a variety of representations for fractions, students should be able to order fractions using informal strategies as opposed to following procedures like changing fractions to common denominators.

- *Considering the reasonableness of solutions when operating with fractions.* Students should be able to use their understanding of the relative size of fractions as a tool to estimate reasonable solutions to fraction operation tasks.

- *Making sense of procedures using different representations.* Students should be given opportunities to make sense of the symbolic procedures for operating with fractions by exploring operations using different representations in ways that lead them to construct meaningful strategies for operating with fractions.

- *Making sense of new models for fractions by building connections to familiar ones.* Students can use their prior understanding of a fraction representation along with other key elements of reasoning and sense making to make sense of new models for fractions.

Process and Practices in Reasoning About Fractions

These key elements of reasoning and sense making with fractions are embedded in the National Council of Teachers of Mathematics Process Standards (NCTM 2000) as well as the Common Core State Standards for Mathematics Content Standards and Mathematical Practices (NGA Center and CCSSO 2010). Elementary students should engage in activities that involve fractions to improve their understanding of fractions as quantities and numbers on a number line. These activities should support their initial understanding of fractions in relation to other numbers. CCSSM Standard for Mathematical Content (SMC) 3.NF.3 suggests that third graders should be able to compare fractions with the same numerator or same denominator by reasoning about their size and to justify their conclusions with visual models. In grade 4, students build on this early understanding of the relative size of fractions and extend their reasoning to include ordering fractions with different numerators and denominators by using benchmarks and justifying their conclusions by using visual models (SMC 4NF.2). In grade 5 students are expected to add and subtract fractions with different denominators using equivalence ideas (SMC 5.NF.1) and to use benchmarks to estimate mentally and assess the reasonableness of answers to fraction tasks (SMC 5NF.2). Fifth graders are expected to apply their extant understanding of multiplication and division with whole numbers to fractions (SMC 5.NF.4 and 5.NF.7). Within these content standards for fraction operations, understanding involves reasoning supported by story contexts and visual models that students use to explain why the operations work as they do.

When students justify conclusions and connect reasoning to visual models they are exhibiting characteristics of the Standards for Mathematical Practice (SMP) 1 and 3: "Make sense of problems and persevere in solving them" and "Construct viable arguments and critique the reasoning of others." Classrooms that encourage students to make and investigate conjectures also reflect the *Principals and Standards for School Mathematics* Process Standards of Reasoning and Proof, Representation, and Connections. As implied in these standards, young children should be given opportunities to express their conjectures in their own words and to use concrete models and other visuals to support their reasoning and communicate their mathematical ideas.

The next sections expand on each key element of reasoning and sense making. The students whose reasoning is shared here learned about fractions in classrooms with teachers who valued broadening mathematical knowledge by problem solving, using multiple representations, building connections among representations, and reasoning and communicating mathematical ideas.

Judging the Relative Size of Fractions

Before judging the relatives size of fractions students need experiences with appropriate representations that build strong mental representations for fractions as numbers. Students should be able to judge the relative size of a fraction based on mental representations for fractions connected to their explorations using concrete models, pictures, and context. For example, students can develop a generalization about the size of a fraction's denominator based on exploring unit fractions using fraction circles, equal-sharing story problems, or paper-folding activities. Students should be able to provide informal explanations and justifications for why $\frac{1}{4} < \frac{1}{3}$ by connecting back to a concrete representation or to their ideas about equal sharing.

Folding paper strips (1-by-8$\frac{1}{2}$–inch strips) is a helpful tool for examining the relationship between the size of each part and the number of parts the whole is divided into. Having students fold paper strips into halves, fourths, eighths, and so on, helps them form the general idea that as the number of parts increase, the size of each part decreases. Teachers can support the students' use of this idea by asking them to compare $\frac{1}{2}$ and $\frac{1}{3}$, $\frac{1}{4}$ and $\frac{1}{8}$, $\frac{1}{10}$ and $\frac{1}{100}$. But teachers should ensure that students consider both parts of the fraction in their explanation. When comparing $\frac{1}{3}$ and $\frac{1}{4}$, students may say that "thirds are bigger because the bottom number is smaller." That information is not enough to compare, for example, $\frac{2}{3}$ and $\frac{1}{4}$. Students should be encouraged to comment on both the numerator and denominator: "Thirds are bigger pieces, and one larger piece is more than one smaller piece."

Research on children's thinking suggests that students can reason about and make generalizations concerning three different types of fraction pairs without relying on symbolic procedures. These pairs are: (a) comparing fractions to $\frac{1}{2}$ or 1, (b) comparing fractions with the same numerator, and (c) comparing fractions like $\frac{3}{4}$ and $\frac{4}{5}$, where the difference between the numerator and denominator of both is the same (Cramer, Post, and delMas 2002; Empson and Levi 2011; Wilson et al. 2011).

The ability of students to construct and use these informal ordering strategies is one indication of fraction number sense. Teachers can use fraction-order tasks based on these three types of fraction pairs to assess whether or not the experiences students have do in fact lead students to reasoning about the relative size or magnitude of fractions. Asking students these types of ordering questions provides them with an opportunity to explain and justify their thinking in ways that go beyond following a procedure. When students are explaining, justifying, and generalizing they are engaging in mathematical reasoning.

Consider, for example, the explanations fourth-grade students provided for the two tasks shown in Example 3.1. The students were asked to name a fraction less than $\frac{1}{2}$ or greater than $\frac{1}{2}$. Avi, Ryan, and Carlos were learning about fractions using fraction-circle pieces (fig. 3.1) that came in different colors for each fractional part (e.g., 2 yellows equal the whole circle; 2 blues equal 1 yellow piece; 9 reds equal 3 blues). At the start of the day's lesson, the teacher asked the students order questions to see if at that point in their fraction unit they were able to use $1/2$ as a benchmark without using the fraction-circle pieces. The teacher expected the students to be able to explain and justify their responses by making connections to the mental representations that they had constructed for themselves from previous lessons and, that they were building their understanding of fraction magnitude from concrete models that lead to strong mental representations for common fraction amounts.

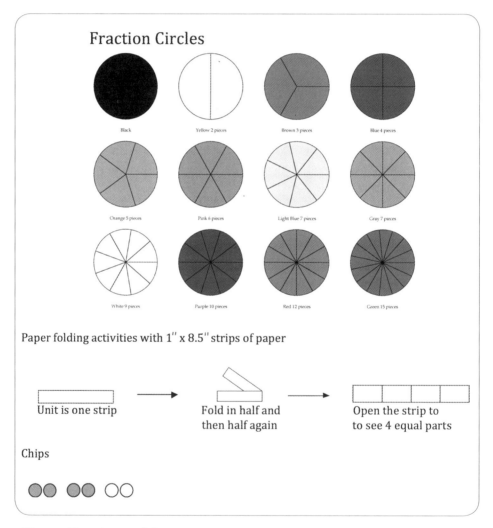

Fig. 3.1. Fraction models

Example 3.1: Judging the Relative Size of a Fraction Using $^1/_2$
as a Benchmark

Task 1: Name a fraction less than $^1/_2$ and explain how you know it is less than $^1/_2$.

Avi: $^1/_4$ is less than $^1/_2$. If you put a blue piece over 1 yellow, you would still see some yellow.

Ryan: $^1/_{12}$. One red piece is less than 1 yellow piece.

Task 2: Name a fraction greater than $^1/_2$ and explain how you know it is greater than $^1/_2$.

Carlos: $^4/_6$ is greater than $^1/_2$. I know that 6 pinks equal the whole circle, so pinks are sixths and half of 6 is 3. So 3 pinks equal $^1/_2$; 4 pinks would be greater than $^1/_2$.

Students can also broaden their understanding of fractions as numbers (as well as magnitudes) by exploring story problems that involve equal sharing (Empson and Levi 2011). Such problems build on students' prior experience with whole number division and provide students with the opportunity to use their intuitive understanding of sharing to reason about the relative size of fractional amounts. Example 3.2 provides an example of equal-sharing story problems and the types of pictures and explanations that children use to make sense of the tasks therein. This example of student work comes from the homework of upper elementary students who were exploring fraction operations using multiple concrete models and different story contexts. The beginning of the fraction operation unit provided students with a review dealing with fraction-order tasks. The key reasoning behind comparing fractions with the same numerator is based on the generalization that the larger the denominator, the smaller each fractional part. This is a fraction generalization that students can construct for themselves with equal-sharing story problems.

Example 3.2: An Equal-sharing Problem and Comparing Fractions
with the Same Numerators

Task 3: Mary shared a large pizza with three other friends and received her fair share. Jose shared a large pizza (same size as Mary's pizza) with two other friends and received his fair share. Who ate more? Why?

Lily:	José and the two other friends did because Mary had gotten $1/4$ of a pizza and José had gotten $1/3$ of a pizza.

Emerson:	José ate more because he had less people to split the pizza with.

The power of mental representations to support students' reasoning ability is further demonstrated in Example 3.3. The same group of fourth graders from Example 3.1 was asked to determine which was larger, $2/3$ or $11/12$, and to do so without using any materials. Example 3.3 is a record of the conversation the teacher and the students had as they reasoned through this task by drawing upon their mental representations for fractions connected to the model used in class.

Example 3.3: Judging the Relative Size of Fractions with Unlike Numerators and Denominators

Task 4: I want you to imagine that the whole circle is our unit. Think about $2/3$. What does it look like? Than imagine $11/12$ of the same circle. Which is bigger, $2/3$ or $11/12$?

Cole:	$2/3$ covers up 2 parts out of 3 parts. 11 parts out of 12 parts is more.
Teacher:	You say more? You have to convince me that $11/12$ is more.
Cole:	$11/12$ has more pieces. It will cover up more than $2/3$.
Teacher:	Would anyone else like to add to that picture?
Hannah:	Twelfths are smaller pieces, and there is 1 piece missing. Then it's almost a whole.

Teacher:	But with $^2/_3$, there is 1 piece missing as well.
Hannah:	But the $^1/_3$ is a bigger piece.
Ryan:	The red pieces are the twelfths, and the brown pieces are the thirds. One red piece is smaller than 1 brown piece, so $^2/_3$ leaves a big brown piece open and the red piece is smaller.
Teacher:	With all three explanations you have now convinced me that $^{11}/_{12}$ is bigger than $^2/_3$.

A follow-up question such as "We know that the red piece is smaller than the brown piece, but what does that mean about the amount that is left open?" could have engaged more students in the conversation and helped the teacher determine if other students were convinced that $^{11}/_{12} > ^2/_3$.

Elementary students are able to construct for themselves strategies for comparing fractions that are connected to their exploration using different concrete models. Initial experiences with both story problems and appropriate concrete models support students' development of fraction number sense by building an understanding of the magnitude of common fractions (SMP 2).

But how students judge the relative size of fractions will evolve from relying on mental representations connected to models and context to identifying numerical patterns. In Example 3.4, grade 5 students who explored fractions using fraction circles, paper folding, and story problems involving equal sharing were able to make generalizations about the relationship between the numerator and denominator of fractions to determine if a fraction was greater or less than $^1/_2$. Making generalizations from observed patterns is a form of mathematical reasoning.

These students were able to use $^1/_2$ as a benchmark along with other informal ordering strategies without making an explicit connection to a concrete model as the fourth graders did in Example 3.3. Examples of student thinking shown in Example 3.4 are from a written test in which students were asked to select the larger of two fractions and to order a set of four fractions.

Example 3.4: Judging the Relative Size of a Set of Fractions Using Symbolic Reasoning

Task 5: Circle the larger fraction: $^6/_{14}$ or $^9/_{16}$. Explain your reasoning.

William:	$^9/_{16}$ is greater than $^6/_{14}$ because 9 is over half of 16 but 6 is under half of 14.
Tyler:	$^9/_{16} = ^1/_2 + ^1/_{16}$ is over $^1/_2$ and $^6/_{14} = ^3/_7$; $^3/_7$ is just under $^1/_2$.
Hamdi:	$^9/_{16}$ is more than $^8/_{16}$, which is $^1/_2$, and $^6/_{14}$ is not half; $^7/_{14}$ is.

Task 6: Order the fractions $^4/_5$, $^1/_{10}$, $^7/_{18}$, $^4/_8$ from smallest to largest. Write a list of directions on how to order each set.

Elliot: $^1/_{10}$, $^7/_{18}$, $^4/_8$, and $^4/_5$. I first thought that $^1/_{10}$ was very small compared to the others. And I knew that $^4/_5$ was going to be the biggest, so I took $^7/_{18}$ and figured out that $^7/_{18}$ is less than $^1/_2$ and $^4/_8$ equals $^1/_2$, so I got that.

Alexis: $^1/_{10}$, $^7/_{18}$, $^4/_8$, $^4/_5$. There is only 1 in the numerator for $^1/_{10}$. $^4/_8$ is half (no others are half). 7 is just below half of 18, and 1 more to make 1 for $^4/_5$.

Teachers can use the tasks presented here as formative assessment tools to determine if their instruction is in fact developing students' capacity to construct for themselves these informal reasoning strategies for judging fraction size. If students' first inclination is to change all fractions to common denominators or to use "tricks" like finding cross products of numerators and denominators of the fraction pair, they will be at a disadvantage when judging the reasonableness of answers to fraction-operation problems (Cramer and Wyberg 2007). The experiences students have should support their ability to reason about the magnitude of fractions, as this capability will support student's facility in judging the reasonableness of answers to fraction-operation tasks.

Sample activities that have been shown to support the types of student thinking involved in determining the relative size of fractions are shown in figures 3.2 and 3.3. Figure 3.2 shows examples of activities to use with fraction circles and paper-folding models (www.cehd.umn.edu/ci/rationalnumberproject /rnp1-09.html). Note the last task in figure 3.2. Here students have to consider the role of the unit in comparing fractions. Ordering tasks assume that the unit for each fraction compared is the same. Asking questions that encourage students to consider the role of the unit in comparison tasks is a worthwhile reasoning activity.

Figure 3.3 shows sample equal-sharing story problems that support children's reasoning about the relative size of fractions (Empson and Levi 2011).

Naming Fractions Using the Fraction Circles

I. The black circle is the unit. What fraction name can you give these pieces?

1 yellow _____1-half_____   1 brown _____

1 blue _____   1 gray _____

1 white _____   1 green _____

1 red _____   1 pink _____

Directions: Use fraction circles to fill in the table.			
Color	How many cover 1 whole circle?	Which color takes MORE pieces to cover 1 whole?	Which color has SMALLER pieces?
1. Brown	3		
Orange	5	√	√
2. Orange			
White			
3. Purple			
White			

Use the whole black circle as your unit. Make the fraction $^2/_5$ with the fraction circles. Decide if $^2/_5$ is greater or less than $^1/_2$. Use words to describe the relationship: is less than; is greater than; is equal to. Order the fractions below in the same manner.

$$\frac{2}{3} \quad \boxed{} \quad \frac{1}{2} \qquad\qquad \frac{5}{12} \quad \boxed{} \quad \frac{1}{2}$$

Use paper folding strips to compare two fractions. Circle the larger fraction or both if equal

$\frac{1}{2}$	$\frac{1}{4}$		$\frac{6}{8}$	$\frac{3}{8}$
$\frac{2}{3}$	$\frac{1}{6}$		$\frac{4}{8}$	$\frac{1}{2}$
$\frac{4}{8}$	$\frac{4}{6}$		$\frac{2}{3}$	$\frac{2}{8}$

Jamal and Mara both ate $^1/_2$ of a pizza. Jamal said he ate more than Mara. Mara said that they ate the same amount. Could Jamal be correct? Support your explanation with pictures.

Fig. 3.2. Sample activities to build mental images of fractions and ordering strategies (Rational Number Project: Developing initial fraction ideas using models from fig. 3.1) www.cehd.umn.edu/ci/rationalnumberproject/rnp1-09 .html

Story problem	Task type and size of fraction
4 people want to share 6 brownies so everyone gets the same amount. How much brownie will each child have?	Naming Fractions: Answer >1
4 children want to share 3 small pizzas so everyone gets the same amount. How much pizza can each child have?	Naming Fractions: Answer <1
Who will get more pizza if children share the pizza equally? A child sitting at a table with 3 friends or a child sitting at a table with 2 friends?	Ordering Unit Fractions: Fractions <1
Who gets more candy? A child sharing 3 small bags of candy with 4 children or a child sharing 4 small bags of candy at a table with 8 children?	Ordering Fractions using ½ as benchmark

Fig. 3.3. Fair share story problems for building understanding of fraction magnitude (Empson and Levi 2011)

Considering Reasonableness of Solutions When Operating with Fractions

Understanding how to reason about fractions goes beyond knowing how to use a standard algorithm to find an exact answer. One aspect of reasoning about how to add, subtract, multiply, or divide fractions is the ability to estimate what a reasonable answer would be. The ability to judge the reasonableness of the answer supports students' application of procedures and can act as a guide as to whether the student has applied the procedure correctly. Teachers can have students learn first hand that estimating and judging the reasonableness of answers are valuable endeavors by providing them with a variety of tasks that ask them to do both.

Student work shown in Example 3.5 shows how students might apply their understanding of fraction magnitude to determine if a sum or difference is reasonable. Student responses are from a homework assignment given to the same upper elementary classroom mentioned in Example 3.4. Notice how Travis, Molly, and Camille use ½ as a benchmark, compare unit fractions, and visualize how far away a fraction is from the whole.

Example 3.5: Using Reasoning Based on Informal Ordering Strategies to Judge the Reasonableness of Answers

> *Task 7: Use your estimation skills to determine if the answer is reasonable. Do not find the exact answer. Make your decision based on estimation and describe your reasoning.*

Travis:	$2/3 + 1/4 = 11/12$. Yes, I do think it is reasonable. Because $2/3$ is close to 1 and $1/4$ is close to $1/3$, and if you add them, they are close to 1. Also $11/12$ is close to 1.
Molly:	$8/15 - 1/3 = 7/12$. Eight sixteenths is practically the same thing as $7/12$: both are a little larger than $1/2$. And you are taking away a little bit less than half; so no, it doesn't work!
Camille:	$2/3 - 1/4 = 1/12$. Doesn't make sense; $1/4$ is smaller than $1/3$ and $1/12$ is smaller than $1/4$. More than $1/3$ is left.

Again you can see how the informal ordering strategies (comparing fractions with the same numerator, using $1/2$ as a benchmark, reflecting on fractions close to one) support students' ability to make sense of fraction addition and subtraction tasks. Teachers can extend students' reasoning on these types of estimation tasks by asking them to be more precise in their reasoning. For example when a sixth grader in the same classroom was asked to estimate $2/3 + 1/5$, his response was as follows: "He used more than $1/2$ cup because $2/3$ is more than $1/2$. He used less than 1 cup. Because $1/5$ is less than $1/2$." The teacher responded by asking another question to challenge his thinking: "Why would that be enough to know that the answer is less than 1?" The student then proceeded to reason further about the relative size of the fractions: "Because $1/5$ is 1 out of 5, and so it's smaller pieces." The teacher asked again: "What must you add to $2/3$ for it to be 1 cup?" The student clarified his thinking by comparing the two fractions: "$1/3$ is needed, but $1/3$ is bigger than $1/5$" (Cramer, Wyberg, and Leavitt 2008).

Teachers can also use discussion of students' incorrect reasoning as a way to enhance students' reasoning skills. A common error in estimating fractions is to add the numerators and denominators. A student might say that $2/3 + 1/5$ is $3/8$. The teacher could approach this error as an opportunity to reinforce students' ordering ideas and to model how reasoning about fractions and their relative sizes works. To engage students in a discussion that would help them understand why $3/8$ is an unreasonable answer, the teacher could ask any of the following qustions: "About how big is $2/3$? Is $2/3$ more or less than $1/2$? How big is $1/5$ in comparison to $2/3$? Which is bigger $1/5$ or $1/3$? How many eighths equal $1/2$? Is $3/8$ more or less than $1/2$? How can you use your ideas about the relative size of fractions used in $2/3 + 1/5 = 3/8$ to determine if the answer is reasonable?

Figure 3.4 provides samples of tasks teachers can use to support this type of reasoning. Teachers should purposefully select fractions that would encourage reasoning based on students' informal ordering ideas rather than on rote procedures or rounding. After students work on these types of tasks, teachers can choose from among the different reasoning they observe and have their students present their strategies to the class.

For each problem, imagine the fractions using fraction circles. Estimate the value of each sum or difference. Put an X in the interval where you think the actual answer will be.

$\dfrac{5}{6} + \dfrac{11}{12}$

$\dfrac{4}{7} + \dfrac{6}{11}$

$1\dfrac{1}{4} - \dfrac{1}{3}$

1. After the party, there was 1 full pizza and $^{1}/_{2}$ of another pizza left. Then Brianna ate an amount equal to $^{7}/_{8}$ of a whole pizza. About how much of one pizza was left? More than a whole pizza or less than a whole pizza? More than $^{1}/_{2}$ of pizza or less than $^{1}/_{2}$ pizza?

2. Joshkin ran just over 15 laps of the track; he ran about $15^{3}/_{4}$ laps. His friend ran a little over 14 laps; he ran about $14^{1}/_{3}$ laps. About how much further did Joshkin run? Provide an estimate only.

Estimation and Story Problems: Provide a reasonable estimate with a clear explanation of your thinking. Exact answer is not needed.

Fig. 3.4. Estimation activities that support students' reasoning

Making Sense of Procedures Using Different Representations

Learning to compute with fractions is an opportunity for students to participate in reasoning and sense making. Reys et al. (2012) suggest that "computation is a problem-solving process, one in which children are encouraged to reason their way to answers, rather than merely memorizing procedures that the teacher says are correct" (p. 228). The standard algorithm for fraction division that involves reinterpreting the division problem as a multiplication one with a reciprocal is efficient but not a procedure that is usually meaningful to students. But, by involving students with story problems for division that build on their experiences with whole-number division, students can create models for solving these division-story problems. With guidance from their teacher, students can connect informal models to more sophisticated models and procedures (Gravemeijer and van Galen 2003).

Measurement story problems have been shown to support students' development of a common-denominator process for fraction division (Gregg and Gregg 2007). In measurement division stories, the amount in each group is known, as is the total amount. The number of groups is the missing value. The following division story is a measurement example:

Addis is a baker. She bought 50 pounds of flour. It is easier to use if the flour is repackaged into 5-pound containers. How many containers can Addis make?

The question students need to ask themselves is "How many 5 pounds are in 50 pounds?" Teachers can use the same type of division story but one with fractions. Without direct instruction, students can work together to use pictures to solve similar division stories. With guiding questions from their teacher, students can make connections between their pictures, explain why the pictures solve the task, and familiarize themselves with the common-denominator procedure for dividing fractions. In Example 3.6, Tyler, an upper elementary student explains how he reasoned through a division story problem with a picture.

Example 3.6: Making Sense of Fraction-Division Story Problems

Task 8: You have 4 cups of lemonade concentrate. If you mix $^2/_5$ of a cup with a gallon of water to make a pitcher of lemonade, how many pitchers can you make with 4 cups of concentrate?

Tyler: [*Started out with a picture of 4 whole rectangles*] I made 4 groups of fifths (see fig. 3.5). Then I saw how many groups, how many sets of $^2/_5$ went into each whole.

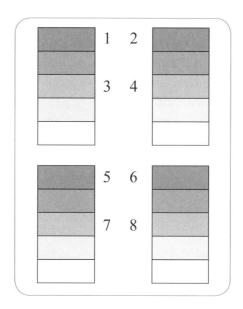

Fig. 3.5

Tyler: There are 8 sets of $^2/_5$ and $^1/_5$ left over in each rectangle. So if you add these one-fifths together, you get another set. So the 8 pitchers you started with and 2 [*the two circled sections of $^2/_5$ in figure 3.6*] equals 10.

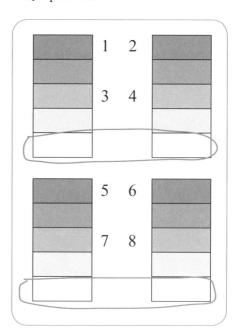

Fig. 3.6

Teacher: Let's look at the original number sentence: 4 ÷ ²/₅. How did Tyler change the 4 whole rectangles? How can we represent that change in the picture with a change in the division sentence?

$$\frac{20}{5} \div \frac{2}{5}$$

Here a teacher can help students see the connection between the change in the picture and the solution strategy of counting out groups of ²/₅. In what way was each whole rectangle changed? As each whole rectangle was partitioned into fifths, the picture shows that 4 equals 20 fifths. The teacher and students can refer to this new number sentence as one that represented the change in the picture, that is, the way the picture was changed to solve the problem.

Connections to the common-denominator procedure should be established cautiously. Initially teachers might guide students to record the change in their pictures with symbols as Tyler did without formalizing the idea that once you have common denominators you only have to pay attention to the numerators. The number sentence acts first as a record of what students constructed pictorially and explained. Through multiple examples, some students will make that observation for themselves. At that time, teachers can do more with that observation to formalize the common-denominator procedure. By looking back at all the problems the class solved and the number sentences that matched the pictures of the solutions, teachers can help students reason about the possible similarities among the problems and how each solution depends on division of the numerators. Students can solve similar problems with this student-constructed procedure and verify their solutions with pictures.

These division problems become more interesting when students have to deal with a remainder. How can students make sense of the remainder in fraction division-story problems? Which fraction concepts related to the role of the unit support students' understanding of the remainder? In Example 3.7, two students, Max and India, discussed how to name the remainder in a fraction-division problem. When the students reconsidered what the unit was, they reached agreement on how to name the remainder.

Example 3.7: Making Sense of the Remainder

Task 9: You have 2¹/₂ pounds of fish. The serving size is ³/₄ pound. How many servings do you have? How can you describe the amount left over?

Max: I drew 2¹/₂. These lines weren't there. I added fourths. There's ³/₄ of a serving so this would be 1 serving, this would be 2 servings, this would be 3 servings, and then it would be 4 servings.

Teacher: But you only have 2¹/₂ pounds of fish

Max: Ok. [*Scribbles out half of the last pound-circle.*] Here's 1, 2, and 3. So it's 3¹/₃.

India: No, it's 3 and ¹/₄. Take the whole and cut it into fourths. It's ¹/₄.

Max: I say it's ¹/₃ because ³/₄ is the serving, and the ¹/₄ piece is ¹/₃ of that.

India: Oh, I get it!

Making sense of the remainder is an important part of using pictures to solve this type of division story. To do so, students need to be flexible in interpreting and making sense of fractional amounts based on different units. When using concrete models like fraction circles, students can be asked to assign to each piece a name that is based on what is used as the unit or whole. A red piece may be named ¹/₆ when a yellow piece is the unit or whole, but ¹/₁₂ when the black circle is the unit or whole. When modeling fractions with chips, 2 chips may be ¹/₄ of a set of 8 chips, but they would be ¹/₆ of a set of 12 chips. Example 3.8 shows how Holly reasoned about the remainder in a fraction-division story problem.

Example 3.8: Making Sense of the Remainder

Task 10: You have 2¹/₆ pints of ice cream from Ben and Jerry's. You are planning on serving each friend ²/₆ of a pint. How many servings can you dish out?

Holly: Since each serving size is ²/₆, you divide the rectangles into sixths, then shade parts. Then figure out that the ¹/₆ left over is ¹/₂ of the serving.

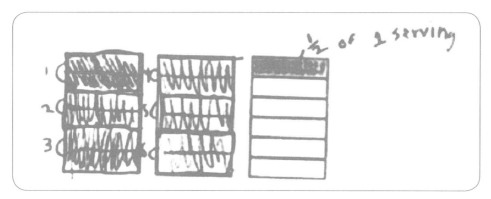

Fig. 3.7

Teaching fraction division by exploring story contexts, pictures, and symbols provides students with the opportunity to build procedural knowledge through reasoning and sense making. Students build meaning for the common-denominator procedure by making connections between stories, pictures, and symbols that were used as records of what students did with the pictures. By examining multiple examples students have the opportunity to generalize their reasoning in a way that leads to a meaningful process for dividing fractions. As students work through examples like those previously presented here, they have many opportunities to explain, justify, and generalize (SMP 2 and 3).

Figure 3.8 shows other division problems that students can solve by drawing pictures and recording their actions with symbols. As students work in groups to complete these tasks, teachers should thoughtfully select students to present their solutions to allow the whole class to witness different correct strategies and any incorrect ones. During this sharing time, the presenters will have an opportunity to reason aloud, offer arguments as to why their strategies work, and develop their language for expressing their ideas (NCTM 2014).

Sophia wants to make as many pans of brownies as she can. Each batch calls for $3/4$ cup of chocolate chips. If Sophia has 2 cups of chocolate chips, how many pans of brownies can she make?
Salma has $4^1/2$ ounces of tea leaves. If $1/4$ of an ounce is needed to make a serving, how many servings of tea can Salma make? Picture this in your mind or draw a picture to solve. Is there a reminder? If so, describe as a fraction.
You have 4 cups of flour. The recipe you are making calls for $2/3$ cup of flour. Estimate: About how many full recipes can you make? At least 4? At least 8? Solve with pictures and represent the remainder as a fraction.
You have $2^1/2$ yards of ribbon. You cut it into pieces $3/4$ in length. Estimate: About how many full pieces can you cut? At least 2? At least 5? Draw a picture to represent the problem. Is there a remainder? If so, describe as a fraction.

Fig. 3.8. Division story problems for building common-denominator approach

Students' work with story problems, pictures, and symbols supports their estimation skills for division. Teachers should encourage students to reason through estimation tasks by relying on the order and equivalence ideas they have been exposed to and on their own mental images of the problems. Consider this problem: You have 4 pounds of candy hearts. You are going to put about $3/4$ pound each into separate baggies. How many bags can you make? Guiding questions to build estimation skills might take the form of the following: If you made 1-pound bags, how many baggies would you make? Is $3/4$ more or less than 1? Does that imply you can make more or fewer than 4 baggies with $3/4$ in each? If you made $1/2$-pound bags, how many baggies would you make (how many halves in 4 can be done mentally)? Is $3/4$ greater or less than $1/2$? Does that mean you can make more than 8 bags or fewer than 8 bags with $3/4$ in each bag? Just as students have learned to use estimating with fraction addition and subtraction, having them use $1/2$ as a benchmark and compare fractions using the informal ordering strategies they construct for themselves also help them reason through division estimation tasks. These skills with fractions exemplify the standard for mathematical practice (SMP 2), "Reason abstractly and quantitatively." Mathematically proficient students make sense of quantities and the relationships among them. Other ways to present estimation tasks are shown in figure 3.9.

You have $2^1/2$ yards of ribbon. You cut it into pieces $3/4$-yard long. Estimate: About how many full pieces can you cut? At least 2? At least 5? Explain your thinking.

Estimate by finding the whole number closest to the exact answer: $3^2/3 \div 1/4$. How many fourths in 3? Is $1/4$ greater or less than $2/3$? Can you get two more fourths out of the $2/3$? Explain your reasoning. What mental images are you using to guide your thinking?

You know that $3^1/2 \div 1/2 = 7$. About how much would $3^1/2 \div 3/4$ be? Is it more or less than 7? Explain your reasoning.

Fig. 3.9. Division estimation tasks

Making Sense of New Models for Fractions by Building Connections to Familiar Ones

Young learners use a variety of representations to develop meaning for mathematical concepts and procedures. As we have seen, students in grades 3–5 can use concrete, pictorial, and contextual representations to build meaning for a fraction as a number and for the relative size of a fraction as well as advance their understanding of why certain procedures with fractions work. But the different representations for fractions are not all of equal for students to interpret.

A sense-making endeavor when using multiple concrete models, for example, is determining how a new model represents fractions in the same way that a previously used model did.

The discrete models for fractions (chips or other counters) are more challenging for students to interpret than continuous models (fraction circles, rectangular regions, and paper lengths) (Behr et al. 1983; English and Halford 1995). Perhaps with a discrete model the unit is less salient than when building a fraction with a continuous model. Or perhaps students' whole-number ideas interfere with interpreting a fraction by using chips. Whatever the case, making sense of the discrete representation for fractions is difficult for students.

A group of students in a fourth grade classroom struggled to make sense of the task asking them to represent $3/4$ of 20 chips (white on one side, green on the other side). Students had prior experiences with fraction reasoning using circular pieces, paper strips, and pictures of rectangles. As the class worked in small groups to complete a set of tasks asking them to represent different fractions with chips, a student in one group said, "I don't get it." The teacher, who was working closely with this group, realized that the student was confused; he did not know if should create groups of 4 chips or put the chips into 4 groups. The teacher asked a series of questions to help the students translate from a familiar model to this new model. As the student reasoned about the similarities, he was able to overcome his difficulty with the chip model.

Example 3.9: Making Sense of a New Model by Connecting to Familiar Model

Task 11: You have used fraction circles and paper-folding strips to represent fractions. Model $3/4$ using the chips. Use 20 chips as your unit. Be ready to explain why your model represents $3/4$.

Ryan: I don't get it!

Teacher: Consider the paper strip as the unit. If you were to show $3/4$ with this paper strip, what would you first have to do? [*Teacher holds up the paper strip shown below.*]

Ryan: I would divide it up into 4 equal parts. [*The teacher does that.*]

Teacher: Now you have 20 chips as your unit. What do you have to do?

Ryan: Put them into 4 groups. [*The student does this by dealing out 1 chip at a time to make 4 equal groups (white side showing).*]

Teacher:	How many groups do you have? To show $^3/_4$ with the paper strip, what do I have to do?
Ryan:	Shade 3 of the 4 parts. [*The teacher does this.*]

Teacher:	Now, what are you going to do with your chips to make an exact copy of the 3 shaded equal parts of my paper strip?
Ryan:	Oh! Flip 3 groups of the 4. [*Ryan flips 3 groups of the four so $^3/_4$ of the chips are green.*]

Ryan was able to make sense of the new, more complex model by connecting it to a familiar one. The purpose of using multiple representations is not just so that students can model fractions using continuous and discrete models. When students reason about how the two models are alike and different, they are able to abstract the common mathematical idea embedded in both models. Similarities between paper strips and chips characterize the part-whole concept; differences between the two models are not relevant to the part-whole idea. Reinterpretation of a mathematical idea from one representation to another is a form of mathematical reasoning. NCTM highlighted the importance of representations and the connections among them when they revised the original Standards document in 2000 to include representation as one of its process standards. When students learn from different representations and pay attention to the connections among them, they are advancing their understanding of the underlying mathematical concepts.

This idea of making sense of new models by connecting them to familiar ones can be extended to reinterpreting procedures developed with multiple representations to another unfamiliar representation. Cramer, Wyberg, and Leavitt (2008) found that fraction circles, story problems, and pictures supported students' construction of the common-denominator procedure for adding and subtracting fractions. They found the number line too complex for students to use when they first began learning about the common-denominator algorithm. But they saw that using the number line after students had made sense of the algorithm with other models provided students with a model that linked their conceptual and procedural understanding for this procedure. Students reinterpreted the procedure using the number line and in doing so reinforced and potentially advanced their understanding of the procedure. Consider this student's reasoning as she reinterpreted how to use the common-denominator procedure on the number line.

Example 3.10: Reasoning on the Number Line

Task 12: Show me how to add ³/₄ + ¹/₆ on the number line but estimate first. [Student had a sheet of paper with multiple number lines (0 to 2) partitioned into either halves, thirds, fourths, sixths, eighths, ninths, tenths, or twelfths.]

Leah:	That would be about 1.
Teacher:	Less than 1 or more than 1?
Leah:	A little less than 1, because ³/₄ is almost 1, and there's ¹/₄ [left]. ¹/₆ is less than ¹/₄, so it couldn't fill it in.
Teacher:	Which number line will you use?
Leah:	I would use twelfths because 4 and 6 go into 12. [Procedural link: 12 is the common denominator, which means she should use the number line partitioned into twelfths. The same number line is used for both fractions; using the same number line partitioned into twelfths is a reinterpretation of what a common denominator is.]
Leah:	So ³/₄ of 12. ¹/₄ of 12 is 3 and 3 × 3 equals 9, so ³/₄ is ⁹/₁₂. [*She puts ⁹/₁₂ on the number line.* (Equivalence on the number line: ³/₄ and ⁹/₁₂ are at the same point.)]
Leah:	I know ¹/₆ equals ²/₁₂, so I add 2 more twelfths [equivalence again]. That's ¹¹/₁₂. That matches my estimate of being a little less than 1.

Asking students to reinterpret fraction operations onto the number line is a reasoning and sense-making activity. Readers are encouraged to use a number line to solve the fraction multiplication tasks in figure 3.10 to see how students can potentially advance their understanding of the multiplication algorithm as they figure out how to model the procedure on a number line. While doing this, consider how students' conceptual and procedural knowledge support their reasoning as they construct solutions on the number line.

Max runs down 46th Street. Each block is $1/3$ of a mile long. He runs $2/5$ of a block before he gets tired and stops.	Use an algorithm to solve the problem.	Use the number line to construct a solution.	Explain how you solved the problem on the number line. What ideas supported your reasoning?
Hannah hikes along the Nature Trail at Mud Lake. The trail is $2/3$ of a mile. She hikes $4/5$ of the trail before she stops to take a picture of a hummingbird with her high-speed Leica camera.			
Ramla sprints $2/3$ of a $1^1/4$-mile track. How much of a mile does she run?			

Fig. 3.10. Reinterpreting fraction multiplication on the number line

Closing

Students in grades 3–5 rely on different representations to make sense of mathematical ideas and to solve problems. The different representations students use to explore fraction ideas play an important role in students' reasoning and sense making. When students can order fractions based on informal strategies connected to visuals and contexts, they then have the tools to determine if an answer to a fraction operation problem is reasonable. When students make connections between a context for fraction division and the equation that models it, students are building conceptual and procedural fluency for division of fractions through problem solving. When students build connections between familiar models and more complex models or use their conceptual and procedural understandings to reinterpret algorithms onto a new model, they are involved in worthwhile reasoning and sense-making activities.

References

Behr, M., R. Lesh, T. Post, and E. Silver. "Rational Number Concepts." In *Acquisition of Mathematics Concepts and Processes,* edited by R. Lesh & M. Landau, pp. 92–127. New York: Academic Press, 1983.

Cramer, K., T. Wyberg and S. Leavitt. (2008). "The Role of Representations in Fraction Addition and Subtraction." *Mathematics Teaching in the Middle School* 13, no. 8 (2008): 490–496.

Cramer, K., and T. Wyberg. "When Getting the Right Answers Is Not Always Enough." In *The Learning of Mathematics: National Council of Teachers of Mathematics Yearbook,* edited by M. Strutchens and W. G. Martin, pp. 205–220. Reston, Va.: NCTM, 2007.

Cramer, K., T. Post, and R. delMas. "Initial Fraction Learning by Fourth- and Fifth-Grade Students: A Comparison of the Effects of Using Commercial Curricula with the Effects of Using the Rational Number Project Curriculum." *Journal for Research in Mathematics Education* 33, no. 2 (2002): 111–144.

Empson, S. B., and L. Levi. *Extending Children's Mathematics: Fractions and Decimals.* Portsmouth, NH: Heinemann Press, 2011.

English, L., and G. S. Halford. *Mathematics Education: Models and Processes.* Mahwah, N.J.: Lawrence Erlbaum Associates, 1995.

Gravemeijer, K., and F. van Galen. "Facts and Algorithms as Aroducts of Students' Own Mathematical Activity." In *A Research Companion to Principles and Standards for School Mathematics,* edited by J. Kilpatrick, W. G. Martin, and D. Schifter, pp. 251–267. Reston, Va.: NCTM, 2003.

Gregg, J. , and D. U. Gregg. "Measure and Fair-sharing Models for Dividing Fractions." *Mathematics Teaching in the Middle Grades* 12, no. 9 (2007): 490–496.

National Council of Teachers of Mathematics. *Principles and Standards for School Mathematics.* Reston, Va.: NCTM, 2000.

National Council of Teachers of Mathematics. *Principles to Actions*: *Ensuring Mathematical Success for All.* Reston, Va.: NCTM, 2014.

National Governors Association Center for Best Practices (NGA Center) and Council of Chief State School Officers (CCSSO). *Common Core State Standards for Mathematics. Common Core State Standards (College- and Career-Readiness Standards and K–12 Standards in English Language Arts and Math).* Washington, D.C.: NGA Center and CCSSO, 2010. http://www.corestandards.org

Reys, R., M. M. Lindquist, D. V. Lambdin, and N. L. Smith. *Helping Children Learn Mathematics,* 10th ed. New York: John Wiley & Sons, Inc., 2012.

Wilson, P. H., C. P. Edgington, K. H. Nguyen, R. C. Pescosolido, and J. Confrey. "Fractions: How to Share Fair." *Mathematics Teaching in the Middle School,* 17 no. 4 (2011): 231–236.

Algebraic Reasoning in Grades 3–5

4

Maria Blanton

Algebra has long been a part of school mathematics in higher grades, but only in recent years have we come to view algebra in the elementary grades as essential to students' mathematical success in later years. Current perspectives on teaching and learning algebra, reiterated recently in the *Common Core State Standards for Mathematics* (NGA Center and CCSSO 2010), maintain that integrating algebra *across all of school mathematics* can provide the coherence and depth necessary for learning algebra with understanding. In turn, this can increase students' chance for mathematical success [Kaput 1998, 2008; National Council of Teachers of Mathematics (NCTM) 1989, 2000]. While this longitudinal approach to algebra promises greater inclusiveness for all students, it also raises practical questions regarding how mathematical content in the elementary grades might integrate algebra in appropriate ways and the nature of children's algebraic thinking that develops from this.

But what do we mean by "algebra" in the elementary grades, that is, *early algebra*? Moreover (and in keeping with the theme of this book) how might we recognize when children in elementary grades are reasoning algebraically? What are characteristics of their thinking? What distinguishes *algebraic* reasoning from other forms of reasoning? How is algebraic reasoning in the elementary grades similar to or different from the algebraic reasoning that might occur in later grades, or in a formal study of algebra? The goal of this chapter is to examine these questions by exploring research-based evidence of how children in grades 3–5 reason algebraically, how classroom practice can support this, and how this work connects to important ways of reasoning mathematically as identified in *CCSSM*'s Standards for Mathematical Practice (SMP) and NCTM's *Principles and Standards* (2000) Process Standards (PS).

This chapter is organized around four critical practices of algebraic reasoning (Blanton et al. 2011; Kaput 2008): (1) *generalizing* mathematical relationships and structure, (2) *representing* generalizations in diverse ways through words, pictures, tables, coordinate graphs, and algebraic symbols (i.e., variable notation),

(3) *justifying* generalizations using grade-appropriate arguments, and (4) *acting on or reasoning* with generalizations as objects themselves. It is worth noting that there are strong connections between these practices and the Standards for Mathematical Practice. The core ideas of the SMP might be condensed as: (1) noticing regularity or structure (SMP 7, 8); (2) representing regularity and structure with precision (SMP 6); (3) constructing appropriate arguments to justify mathematical thinking (SMP 3); (4) making use of and reasoning with structure (SMP 2, 7); and (5) solving problems by modeling situations and using appropriate tools strategically (SMP 4, 5). Items 1–4 map closely to the four practices of algebraic thinking identified here, namely, generalizing, representing, justifying, and reasoning with mathematical structure and relationships. While item 5 is more broadly framed and cuts across the other four items somewhat, it, too, captures important aspects of reasoning algebraically. These connections will be more explicitly identified later in this chapter.

In addition this chapter explores these algebraic thinking practices by drawing from three significant content areas in which early algebraic reasoning occurs: (1) generalized arithmetic, (2) relationships between or among quantities, and (3) functional thinking.

Generalized arithmetic involves generalizing arithmetic relationships, including properties of number and operation, as well as reasoning with these relationships to facilitate arithmetic thinking. *Relationships between or among quantities* includes developing a relational understanding of the equals sign, representing and reasoning with expressions and equations in their symbolic form, and describing relationships between and among generalized quantities that may or may not be equivalent. *Functional thinking* includes generalizing relationships between quantities that vary in relation to each other, representing those relationships in multiple ways, and reasoning fluently with these representations in order to interpret and predict function behavior (Blanton et al. 2011).

Because much of early algebra research has crystallized around these areas, they offer a pragmatic framework for discussing algebraic reasoning in a fairly comprehensive way. In what follows, this chapter explores the four practices of algebraic reasoning—generalizing, representing, justifying, and reasoning with mathematical structure and relationships—within these three content areas.

Algebraic Reasoning as a Practice of Generalizing

Generalizing is at the heart of algebraic reasoning (Kaput 2008) and is central to what distinguishes algebraic reasoning from other forms of reasoning. It involves noticing structure and relationships. Developing the practice of generalizing in the elementary grades is critical because it draws children's thinking away from the particulars of arithmetic, where the focus is often on computations with specific numbers or reasoning about particular instances. Instead, it focuses children's attention to how particular instances are related, so that they begin to attend to relationships and structure. Engaging in this practice of generalizing requires students to understand a situation, connect it to their existing knowledge, and draw conclusions (in the form of a generalization), all of which are critical features of reasoning and sense making (NCTM 2009).

Generalized Arithmetic

Because arithmetic is central to mathematics in the elementary grades, one of the more natural starting points for the practice of generalizing is with arithmetic relationships. This involves reasoning about the structure of arithmetic expressions rather than their computational value. One important way this can occur is through noticing the underlying structure or regularity in operations on numbers, that is, generalizing the fundamental properties of number and operation.[1] For example, children might notice that any number multiplied by 1 yields that same number (a generalization known as the multiplicative identity property), or that any number subtracted from itself yields 0 (a generalization known as the additive inverse). Because these properties govern how operations behave and relate to one another (Blanton et al. 2011), they provide a rich arithmetic context in which children can begin to reason algebraically.

The following task (Blanton, Stephens et al. 2015) illustrates this point:

> *Task 1: Marcy's teacher asks her to solve 23 + 15. Marcy adds the two numbers and gets 38. The teacher then asks her to solve 15 + 23. Marcy already knows the answer without adding.*

(a) How do you think Marcy knew the answer without adding again?

(b) Will Marcy's idea always work? Explain why.

(c) Write an equation using variables (letters) to represent the idea that you can add two numbers in any order and get the same result.

With Marcy's task, children might initially compute 23 + 15 and 15 + 23 to make sense of the problem, but as their attention is directed to the behavior of operations on numbers with this structure (that is, of the form $a + b$ and $b + a$), they notice that the order of the addends does not matter. The sums will be the same. This act of noticing an underlying structure is an important aspect of algebraic reasoning.

Generalizing should also involve thinking about the domain for which a generalization holds true; that is, children are reasoning algebraically not only when they notice regularity or structure in operations on numbers but also when they see and are able to characterize the extent to which that structure holds. For example, they not only notice that when the order of two factors is reversed, their product is the same as with the original order—a generalization we refer to as the commutative property of multiplication—they also understand that this property holds for *all* numbers in the number domains they have encountered. Children who do not understand the generality of a claim might notice the underlying structure but think that the claim holds for only isolated instances, such as those numerical cases they might have checked through computational work.

Research indicates that, with support, children are able to notice regularities in operations on numbers and articulate generalizations about their observations (Schifter 2009). For example, in a recent study in grades 3–5 classrooms where instruction was designed to systematically develop children's algebraic reasoning skills, researchers found that students were more likely to notice the underlying structure of the commutative property of addition at play in Marcy's task and to recognize that the generalization worked for "all numbers" than were students who had had only arithmetic-focused instruction (Blanton, Stephens et al. 2015).

In addition to the fundamental properties, there are other opportunities in the study of arithmetic for children to reason algebraically through generalizing. For example, children are reasoning algebraically when they develop generalizations about classes of numbers, such as even numbers and odd numbers. As children operate on such numbers, they notice regularities that allow them to generalize important relationships. In her third-grade classroom, Mrs. Gardiner gave students the following question to explore in groups and asked them to develop a conjecture to represent their thinking:

> *Task 2: Jesse is adding two even numbers. Do you think his answer will be an even number or an odd number?*

The following conversation occurred:

Teacher: Remember, when you are developing your conjecture, you want to think about *all* numbers. When you are ready to write a conjecture about an even plus an even, ask yourselves if this conjecture that you have developed will work *all* the time. How do you think we should start thinking about this?

Mia: I think we should try some math facts, like 2 + 2 is 4. Or maybe we can go back to our cubes and show it that way, like this (*Mia arranges her cubes in the following array to represent 2 + 2*):

So, I think an even plus an even will be an even.

Teacher:	Great, so how would you write that? Let's put together a conjecture.
Jeffrey:	We could say that when you add an even number plus an even number the sum will be even.
Teacher:	I love that! [*She writes it on the board.*]

As with the fundamental properties, generalizing arithmetic relationships such as these also entails understanding that the relationship holds across some domain of numbers, not just in particular instances. To develop this way of thinking, Mrs. Gardiner encouraged children to develop a conjecture (generalization) and to question whether or not it would hold for all numbers. ("Remember, when you are developing your conjecture, you want to think about *all* numbers . . . you want to ask yourselves if this conjecture that you have developed will work *all* the time.")

Relationships Between or Among Quantities

Generalizing is not limited to noticing an underlying structure, such as that in arithmetic properties, but includes generalizing the quantities that constitute these relationships. The following Piggy Bank problem (Blanton, Stephens et al. 2015) provides a way to engage children in reasoning algebraically about relationships between quantities:

> **The Piggy Bank Problem.** Tim and Angela each have a Piggy Bank. They know that their Piggy Banks each contain the same number of pennies, but they don't know how many. Angela also has 8 pennies in her hand.
>
> (a) How would you represent the number of pennies Tim has?
>
> (b) How would you represent the total number of pennies Angela has?
>
> (c) Angela and Tim combine all of their pennies to buy some candy. How would you represent the total number of pennies they have?

Children are reasoning algebraically when they recognize an unspecified quantity (a quantity that has not been assigned a specific numerical value) in a problem situation as a generalized quantity and understand that such quantities do not need to have a known, specific value. For example, in the Piggy Bank problem, children are reasoning algebraically when they recognize that Tim's number of pennies is an unknown quantity that could have any value. In solving this task, third grader Jackson described Tim's number of pennies as P, where P represented "the number of pennies in Tim's bank." Jackson's response to (b) was to represent Angela's number of pennies as $P + 8$. In other words, he recognized that the number of pennies that Tim and Angela each had was both unknown *and* related. He captured their relationship by representing the number of pennies in each of their banks with the same letter, *P*. The point here is that Jackson *noticed* a generalized (unknown) quantity, an action inferred from the fact that he accurately represented this the number of pennies Tim and Angela each had.

Children who cannot reason algebraically have a great deal of difficulty representing either Tim's or Angela's number of pennies because each reflects an unspecified quantity. Instead, they typically assign a specific value to these unknown quantities (Carraher, Schliemann, and Schwartz 2008), even though it violates the problem situation. Such thinking is not surprising; mathematics instruction that focuses on arithmetic—and that excludes algebraic reasoning—can promote the misconception in children's thinking that all quantities must be specific, known values. However, it is important for children to have experiences with both generalizing a quantity and noticing a generalized quantity, such as a varying number of pennies, as an object in an expression or an equation or inequality relationship.

Tasks such as the Piggy Bank problem can also be designed to help children reason algebraically about relationships between generalized quantities, whether in the form of equations or inequalities. For example, if children are asked to describe how the number of pennies Tim has relates to the number of pennies that Angela has, they are being asked to reason algebraically about the relationship between two generalized quantities that are not equivalent.

If we are given additional information in the problem that Angela has a total of, say, 12 pennies, we have now constrained the problem so that the unknown number of pennies Angela and Tim each have is now fixed; that is, the quantities are no longer unknown, varying quantities. When children are then asked to describe, for example, what they now know about this new information and the number of pennies Angela has, they are being asked to notice that two quantities representing Angela's number of pennies—one given by "12" and one given by an algebraic expression such as "$P + 8$"—are equivalent to each other and that this relationship can be represented mathematically as $12 = P + 8$.

Seeing relationships between unknown quantities is difficult for children whose mathematical experience has focused exclusively on quantities with specific, known values and who, subsequently, have not learned to reason algebraically with generalized quantities. Research shows, however, that children who have routine experiences with tasks such as the Piggy Bank problem can develop a rich understanding of generalized quantities and the relationships between them (Blanton, Stephens et al. 2015; Dougherty 2008, 2010).

Functional Thinking

In its Algebra Standard, NCTM's *Principles and Standards* (2000) maintains that students across prekindergarten–grade 12 should be able to "understand patterns, relations, and functions" (p. 37). As this statement suggests, functional thinking can serve as an important entry point into early algebra because of its close connection to algebraic reasoning practices (Carraher and Schliemann 2007). Generalizing relationships between two quantities that vary in relation to each other is not only a central component of functional thinking but also an important characteristic of algebraic reasoning. Children are generalizing when they notice how one quantity varies in relation to another quantity *in general.* For example, reasoning inductively from a set of numerical cases, children might notice that the number of wheels on a bicycle is always double the number of bicycles, regardless of the number of bicycles. As Kilpatrick, Swafford, and Findell (2001) point out, children in elementary grades "can observe that over time and across different circumstances, numerical quantities can vary in principled ways. . . . They can learn about functions by studying how a change in one variable is reflected in the behavior of another" (p. 280).

In a recent study (Blanton, Brizuela et al. 2015), children in K–grade 2 were asked to solve the following problem.

> **The Growing Train Problem.** A train engine ran the same route everyday. As it went along, it picked up two cars at each stop.
>
> 1. Not counting the engine, how many cars did it have at stop 1? How many cars did it have at stop 2? How many cars did it have at stop 3? (Assume the train had only the engine prior to stop 1.)
>
> 2. Organize your information. Write an equation that shows the relationship between the values in your table for each pair of values.
>
> 3. Find a relationship between the number of stops and the total number of cars on the train.
>
> 4. In your own words, how would you describe the relationship you found?
>
> 5. Write an equation (rule) to represent your relationship.
>
> 6. Do you think your rule will always work? Why?
>
> 7. If we also count the engine, how would this affect the values in your table? How would this affect your rule?

As first grader Rebecca[2] solved the problem, she represented the relationship between the first stop and the total number of cars as $1 + 1 = 2$, between the second stop and the total number of cars as $2 + 2 = 4$, and between the third stop and the total number of cars as $3 + 3 = 6$ (fig. 4.1). Reasoning inductively from these cases, she noticed—or generalized—a functional relationship between the number of stops and the total number of cars *for any number of cars.*

As with generalizing in other contexts, generalizing functional relationships is a process of reasoning and sense making. Rebecca needed to make sense of a problem situation, that is, the relationship between the number of stops and the total number of train cars, by connecting it to the existing information she had captured in her equations representing the specific cases (e.g., 2 + 2 = 4). She then had to reason about any regularity across the different cases and draw a conclusion in the form of a generalized functional relationship. In this sense, the study of functions provides children with an important way to bridge arithmetic reasoning about particular cases with algebraic reasoning about generalized functional relationships.

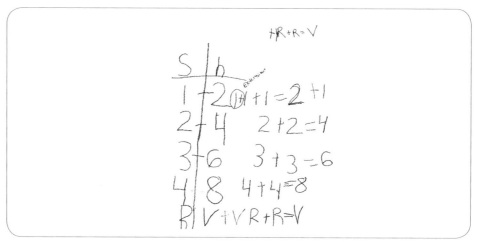

Fig. 4.1. Rebecca's written work on the Growing Train problem

Connections to Curricular Standards

NCTM's *Principles and Standards* (2000) has long supported the practice of generalizing as part of its algebra strand. It maintains that children in grades 3–5 should be able to "describe, extend, and *make generalizations* [emphasis added] about geometric and numeric patterns," identify the fundamental properties and "use them to compute with whole numbers," and "investigate how a change in one variable relates to a change in a second variable." Generalizing, itself, involves the act of making a conjecture—the basis of the Reasoning and Proof Process Standard (PS 2)—as students describe what they notice.

In conjunction with NCTM's *Principles and Standards* (2000) and building on the Process Standards, the CCSSM states that mathematically proficient students should be able to "make sense of quantities and their relationships"

(SMP 2), "look for and make use of structure" (SMP 7), and "look for and express regularity in repeated reasoning" (SMP 8). When children generalize, they are engaged in these essential practices. For example, as children generalize arithmetic relationships such as the fundamental properties, they are looking for regularity in how operations behave (SMP 8b) and noticing the underlying structure (SMP 7a). As children model problem situations with generalized quantities through expressions, equations, or inequality relationships, such as those of the Piggy Bank problem, they are abstracting a given situation (SMP 2b) to identify important (generalized) quantities and to look for relationships between these quantities (SMP 7). Finally, as they generalize functional relationships, they are reasoning about quantities and their relationships (SMP 2a). As noted earlier, Rebecca reasoned about how quantities in her table were related and was able to characterize relationships between two specific values in a pair (e.g., 2 + 2 = 4 for the pair [2, 4]; SMP 4a). Moreover, she was also able to decontextualize by looking across a set of specific cases to abstract a general relationship (SMP 2b, 3e, 4c).

Algebraic Reasoning as a Practice of Representing Generalizations

Although generalizing might be described as the heart of algebraic reasoning, it remains hidden without representations to bring children's thinking to light. Children are reasoning algebraically as they represent mathematical generalizations—whether it be in words, tables, coordinate graphs, pictures, or variable notation—and navigate between these representations. Moreover, their representations are not only evidence of the generalizations they notice in problem situations, but the action of representing helps shape the very nature of their knowledge about algebraic concepts. Morris (2009) notes, for example, that the act of representing generalized quantities helps children to understand that an action applies to an infinite set of objects, not just a single case. This, in turn, can help strengthen their understanding of the general nature of a claim, which is an important attribute of generalizing.

As part of its Representation Standard, NCTM's *Principles and Standards* (2000) describes that, across all content, students in prekindergarten–grade 12 should be able to—

- create and use representations to organize, record, and communicate mathematical ideas;
- select, apply, and translate among mathematical representations to solve problems; and
- use representations to model and interpret physical, social, and mathematical phenomena (p. 67).

In early algebra, we are interested in how children use diverse representations to characterize structure and relationships. For example, how do they use variable notation to represent generalizations such as function rules or fundamental properties? How does their natural language relate to their use of variable notation? Can they interpret the meaning of a symbolic representation of a problem situation in their own words? Do they understand the connections between how data are represented in function tables as opposed to coordinate graphs? Or, can they understand what features of a table or graph signal a linear relationship? The following section explores how children reason algebraically through the practice of representing the mathematical structure and relationships they notice.

Generalized Arithmetic

As children explore fundamental properties, they often naturally represent their generalizations in words. For example, they might represent the commutative property of multiplication as "You can multiply two numbers in any order and still get the same answer." Because it is a familiar representational system, children's natural language is an important means of scaffolding their development of more sophisticated representations. As accessible as natural language is for discussing mathematical ideas, however, it can be cumbersome as a way to represent arithmetic generalizations (e.g., describing the distributive property of multiplication over addition in words can be difficult). In fact, research suggests that, with appropriate instruction, children not only *can* begin to represent generalizations using variable notation (Cai, Ng, and Moyer 2011; Dougherty 2008; Schliemann, Carraher, and Brizuela 2007), but can sometimes do so more easily than with natural language (Blanton, Brizuela et al. 2015; Blanton, Stephens et al. 2015).

In Marcy's task (fig. 4.1), children are reasoning algebraically as they represent the commutative property of addition in their own words (e.g., "You can add two numbers in either order, and the result will be the same.") or with variable notation (e.g., $a + b = b + a$, where a and b are taken to represent any numbers the children have encountered). In other words, generalizing—here, the process of noticing the underlying behavior of the operation—culminates in a representation that captures that behavior.

With appropriate instruction, students in elementary grades *can* represent such properties—and other generalizations—using variable notation. In one third-grade classroom, students were asked to represent the commutative property of addition using variable notation. Prior to this point in the lesson, these students had engaged with computational work designed to prompt their noticing of this underlying structure and to form a conjecture, in their own words, about what they noticed. They described their conjecture as "You can add the same numbers in any order and get the same result." The teacher then asked students to represent their conjecture with variables. (They had been introduced to variable notation in the previous lesson.) Building on the equation $5 + 6 = 6 + 5$, which the teacher had written on the board earlier, two students suggested that the property could be represented with letters and numbers as $5 + t = t + 5$ and $j + 6 = 6 + j$, respectively. After a conversation in which the children reasoned that these equations were true for all values of the variables, the following exchange took place:

Teacher: Is there a way that we could write an equation about the commutative property using only letters?

Ava: $J + b \ldots$

Teacher: $J + b \ldots$

Ava: Equals $j + b$.

Teacher: Want to think about that one again? You're so close . . .

Ava: Oh, I mean $b + j$.

Teacher: Good. Because we want to show that it's switched around, right? So $j + b = b + j$. Is this a good representation of what our conjecture was? I'm seeing a lot of thumbs up. (Students gave a thumbs-up to indicate agreement.)

Children's reasoning here reflected a useful iterative approach whereby they first represented only one number as a generalized quantity (e.g., $t + 5 = 5 + t$). Ava was then able to build on this reasoning and students' representations to represent the commutative property usiing variable notation.

This understanding of how to represent a generalization requires students to reason algebraically with general quantities and their relationship. For example, to represent the relationship symbolically, children need to understand whether the quantities are general quantities or particular numbers. They also need to understand that the same quantity should be represented consistently with the same symbol and that different quantities should be represented with different symbols. Representing the commutative property of addition, for example, as $a + b = c + d$ is problematic because it does not accurately convey the behavior of the operation. This choice in how to characterize a generalization requires reasoning with the representation itself.

Relationships Between or Among Quantities

Representing generalizations requires prerequisite knowledge that can be developed within the study of arithmetic. One of the most critical concepts children should develop is a relational understanding of the equals sign (Carpenter, Franke, and Levi 2003). Because many generalizations are represented mathematically in the form of an equation (e.g., function rules, fundamental properties), it is critical that children understand that the equals sign denotes a relationship of equivalence so that they can accurately represent problem situations in early algebra (and also in arithmetic). Students who have this *relational* view of the equals sign are able to think flexibly about the relationship between quantities in an equation. In contrast, students who have only an *operational* view of the equals sign interpret this symbol as "compute the expression to the left of the equals sign and record the answer immediately after it" (Carpenter, Franke, and Levi 2003). Such students will be hard pressed to construct equations to represent problem situations that are not represented in a standard format (e.g., $3 + 5 = 8$).

Although the equals sign is addressed in CCSSM in first grade, an accurate, relational understanding of this symbol is still problematic for children in upper elementary grades and even beyond. Prior to instruction in one third-grade classroom that was designed to develop students' relational thinking about the equals sign, students described what they thought this symbol meant:

Christa: Say, like, you had 5 and 10. Then you add these two together, and that would be what you get when you add them together.

Kim: It's like your answer.

Martin: It's like the sum.

While these students held an operational view of the equals sign, Robert expressed a different view:

Robert: It can also be like, if things are the same. If you had 35 and 35, that would be equal.

Robert's view reflects a relational understanding of the equals sign that is critical for representing, and ultimately reasoning with, relationships between quantities. For example, perhaps one of the more common aspects of algebraic reasoning involves reasoning with equations to find unknown values. Students who think operationally about the equals sign will find it difficult to represent equivalent quantities with an equation and to find unknowns because they don't view equations holistically, but rather parse them left to right. For example, in a simple equation such as $4 + 7 = \_\_\_ + 8$, children who think operationally will claim that the missing value is either 11 (i.e., $4 + 7$) or 19 (i.e., $4 + 7 + 8$). Students need strategies based on a relational understanding of the equals sign with which they can accurately represent equations to reason about unknown values.

Representing generalizations also requires students to be able to represent generalized quantities as algebraic expressions. For example, in the Piggy Bank problem (p. 71), children need to represent the unknown number of pennies that Tim and Angela each have. Children who cannot reason algebraically about general quantities will represent the number of pennies Tim and Angela each have as a specific numerical value or as a range of specific values (Carraher,

Schliemann, and Schwartz 2008) but not as a general quantity. For example, in a recent study in which third-grade students were given the Piggy Bank problem, some assigned a value of 8 to Tim's number of pennies (Blanton, Stephens et al. 2015).

However, research shows that with appropriate instruction children in elementary grades—even as early as kindergarten—can reason algebraically by representing generalized quantities in both words and variable notation in meaningful ways (Blanton et al. 2015; Carraher et al. 2006). For example, in one first-grade classroom, students were introduced to variable notation as a way to represent unknown quantities. The following excerpt shows first grader Ella talking about how she would represent the unknown number of candies that another child, Madeline, has (Brizuela et al. 2016):

Teacher:	Madeline has a box of candy. We don't know how many pieces are in it, and her friend gives her one more piece of candy. What can you tell me about the number of pieces of candy that Madeline has in her box?
Ella:	Hmm . . . Let me think—*a* plus 1 equals *b*.
Teacher:	Can you write this down for me? And tell me what it means?
Ella:	I meant to do another one.
Teacher:	OK. Just write down what you wanted to say.
Ella:	*E* plus one equals *m*. [*Ella writes e + 1 = m.*]
Teacher:	Tell me about this equation that you've written.
Ella:	*E* plus one equals *m*.
Teacher:	What is *E*?
Ella:	The number that she had in her box and the one is the one that her friend gave her. I put the *m* there [*pointing to the* m *in her equation*], because if you add an *e* it would be the same number. But if you take another letter, you would get another number.
Teacher:	So you're saying you chose a different letter here [*pointing to the* m].
Ella:	Yes.
Teacher:	Because it was . . .
Ella:	To represent it was another number.
Teacher:	So, as I understand it, the *E* represents the number of pieces of candy in the box.
Ella:	Yes.
Teacher:	You added one [piece of candy] on top.
Ella:	For her friend.
Teacher:	Right.

Ella:	And the *m* is for all she has together, but the *E* stands for the number she had without the candy from her friend and the one is from the friend, the candy that the friend gave her. And the *m* is from how much there is.
Teacher:	All together?
Ella:	Yes.

Ella clearly recognizes the generalized quantity in the problem (the unknown number of candies in Madeline's box) and understands how to represent it. Moreover, she understands how to represent the total amount of candies Madeline has and why representing this total amount requires a symbol different from the one used to represent the number of candies in the box.

With the Piggy Bank problem, children might describe the number of pennies that Angela has in comparison to Tim as "Angela has eight more pennies than Tim." With instructional support, they can learn to represent the number of pennies that Tim and Angela each have with variable notation (e.g., Jackson represented Tim's number of pennies as P and chose a related representation for Angela's number of pennies as $P + 8$). This choice of symbolic representation here is strategic. It requires that children make sense of the problem and understand that their representations need to convey the relationship between the quantities, that is, that Tim and Angela have the same number of pennies in their banks but that Angela has 8 more pennies than Tim. Representing the number of pennies Tim has in his bank as P and the total number of pennies Angela has as $S + 8$ (given P in Tim's bank and S in Angela's bank), for example, does not fully capture that relationship.

The significance of tasks like the Piggy Bank problem is that they help children confront their deeply held arithmetic notions about the nature of quantities, namely, that they must be specific, known values. In doing so, children learn to accept the ambiguity of representing—and ultimately reasoning with—quantities whose values are not known, a critical aspect of algebraic reasoning. Moreover, as they represent such quantities using symbolic notation, teachers can help scaffold children's thinking so that they come to understand that the symbol represents a quantity, such as the number of pennies Tim has, and not an object, such as a penny. Children who cannot reason algebraically are likely to experience object/quantity confusion and as a result will view a variable as representing the object itself, not an attribute about the quantity being measured (e.g., Knuth et al. 2005).

Children are reasoning algebraically as they represent relationships between generalized quantities in the form of equations and inequalities. For example, in the Piggy Bank problem, children might represent a relationship between the number of pennies Tim has and the number Angela has as "Angela has 8 more pennies than Tim," or as $P + 8 > P$, given that the number of pennies they each have in their banks is represented by *P*. The representation of these relationships is foundational to algebra not only because they include variable expressions but also because they depict interactions between quantities in generalized forms (Dougherty 2008).

Moreover, when we constrain the problem by providing more information about the number of pennies, children can represent a resulting relationship between the quantities with an equation. For example, if it were known that Angela had 12 pennies, then we could represent this information as $P + 8 = 12$. Modeling a problem situation in such a way involves algebraic reasoning because it requires that children reason with a generalized quantity as well as understand that the relationship between two equivalent quantities can be depicted mathematically by an equation. Understanding that two distinct representations of the same quantity (e.g., the number of pennies Angela has represented as either 12 or $P + 8$) must be equal to each other and that this relationship can be conveyed mathematically as an equation is a sophisticated act of algebraic reasoning for young children.

Functional Thinking

Research shows that children can represent generalized functional relationships using words, tables, coordinate graphs, and variable notation (e.g., Brizuela and Alvarado 2010; Brizuela and Earnest 2008; Tierney and Monk 2008) and that children's use of representations can mediate their understanding of functions (Blanton and Kaput 2004; Brizuela and Lara-Roth 2002). Recent studies suggest, furthermore, that children in classrooms that systematically develop algebraic thinking can represent functions more successfully using variable notation than they can using their own words (Blanton, Stephens et al., 2015) and that, as early as kindergarten, children can successfully use variable notation to characterize functional relationships (Brizuela et al. 2015). In other words, *all* of these forms of representations—words, tables, coordinate graphs, and variable notation—are important tools that children can begin to use to reason algebraically.

First grader Rebecca represented her thinking in both words and variable notation as she solved the Growing Train problem. Reasoning inductively about her set of arithmetic equations (see her written work in fig. 4.1), she noticed a general relationship between the number of stops and the total number of train cars, which she first represented as $R + R = V$. She explained her representation:

Teacher: What does *R* represent in your equation?

Rebecca: *R* represents how many stops the car, the train makes.

Teacher: OK, and what does *V* represent?

Rebecca: How many cars he has.

Teacher: How would you explain this rule to your friend?

Rebecca: Whatever number, how many stops it made, if you doubled it, that's how many cars it would have.

Rebecca was able not only to use both words and symbols to represent her generalization but also to move between these representations by interpreting the meaning of her symbolic rule in her own words.

Another representation Rebecca used was a function table, an important tool that helped her record and organize data, thereby supporting her reasoning about the relationship in "Growing Train." In particular, the table kept the corresponding values for specific numerical cases (e.g., for 3 train stops there were 6 cars) visible, which in turn helped Rebecca notice a "doubling" relationship. With this understanding, she was able to write an equation for each specific case that related the corresponding values (e.g., $3 + 3 = 6$ for the corresponding values 3 and 6) and then reason inductively from these cases to generalize the underlying relationship. In this sense, the function table representation was a critical tool that helped Rebecca recognize the mathematical relationship in Growing Train.

Connections to Curricular Standards

The importance of using diverse representations to model mathematical ideas is clearly indicated in current curricular frameworks. As described earlier, NCTM's *Principles and Standards* (2000) strongly advocates the use of diverse representations and an understanding of how to navigate between them in its Representation Process Standard (PS 5). In its algebra strand, it advocates that children in grades 3–5 should be able to "use representations such as graphs, tables, and equations to draw conclusions," "represent the idea of a variable as an unknown quantity using a letter," and "express mathematical relationships using equations," much as Rebecca did with Growing Train.

In conjunction with these goals, the *Standards for Mathematical Practice* (NGA Center and CCSSO 2010) argues that children should be able to represent relationships between quantities "using such tools as diagrams, two-way tables, graphs, flowcharts and formulas" (SMP 1, 4), to "explain correspondences between equations, verbal descriptions, tables and graphs . . . and search for regularity and trends" and "communicate precisely to others" (SMP 1, 4, 6). Rebecca exhibited these and other practices with Growing Train. She not only used words and symbols to represent the relationship in the problem situation, she also used a function table as a tool to reason inductively about a general relationship (SMP 5). Moreover, she was able to contextualize her symbolic representation, $R + R = V$, by explaining in her own words what it meant in terms of the problem context (SMP 2c): "Whatever number, how many stops it made, if you doubled it, that's how many cars it would have." It is also worth noting the precision with which Rebecca represented her rule, that is, as an equation representing a relationship between two quantities and not as an expression (SMP 6b), as well as her ability to communicate the meaning of her symbolic representation in her own words (SMP 6a).

The activity of using multiple representations and navigating fluently between them is important because different representations necessarily highlight or conceal various aspects of a situation. Moreover, because different representations are accessible to different groups of students, they may serve as a sense-making bridge to more sophisticated representations. Thus, mathematical thinking—and algebraic reasoning—is enriched when more than one representation is used and connections between them are made (Brizuela and Earnest 2008).

Algebraic Reasoning as a Practice of Justifying Generalizations

The *Common Core State Standards for Mathematics* states that students learn to reason mathematically "not by learning vocabulary, but by making conjectures, presenting explanations, and/or constructing arguments," practices that align deeply with early algebra's practices of generalizing, representing, and justifying conjectures about mathematical relationships or structure. As previously described, children are reasoning algebraically when they notice and represent generalizations. In essence, they are making conjectures about structure and relationships. Their algebraic reasoning is sharpened, however, when they extend these practices to *justifying* why a generalization might be true. In early algebra, the practice of justifying a generalization prompts children to think more critically about the underlying behavior in the relationship or structure noticed and to look for clues in contexts and problem data. But there are long-term dividends as well. As Morris (2009) argues, the development of children's capacity to notice and justify relationships about generalized quantities is consistent with the nature of mathematical proof and therefore can help prepare children for a more formal study of proof[3] in later grades. As such, justifying generalizations is an important act of algebraic reasoning.

There is a subtle distinction here that makes justifying a generalization a form of *algebraic* reasoning as opposed to, say, arithmetic reasoning. For example, suppose that the Growing Train problem only asked children to find the total number of train cars if a train made three stops. Through an arithmetic process that might involve drawing pictures and counting, a child could make a convincing argument that the solution is 6 cars. While this type of arithmetic thinking is important, it does not require reasoning with or about a generalized relationship—that is, algebraic reasoning—in developing an argument.

In the practice of justifying generalizations, children are engaged in making grade-appropriate arguments to explore the truth of a generalization (SMP 3g). Over time and with relevant instruction, their arguments can evolve toward more general and sophisticated forms. Carpenter, Franke, and Levi (2003) describe three levels of justification that children make in forming mathematical arguments: (1) appealing to an authority figure (e.g., a conjecture is true because "the teacher said so"), (2) examining particular examples or cases, or (3) building generalizable arguments. The most common type of argument children initially construct is likely one from level 2, an empirical argument whereby they check a set of numerical cases as the basis for their justification. However, research has shown that children can learn to develop more sophisticated general arguments. One such argument is a "representation-based" one, in which children's justifications are based on reasoning with a representation, such as a drawing or a set of objects, rather than a set of specific numerical cases (Schifter 2009). Another type of more general argument involves using generalizations previously established by students to justify a new claim. We will examine these different types more closely in this section.

Generalized Arithmetic

Children often use empirical arguments to justify arithmetic generalizations. For example, they might reason about questions such as "Why does the commutative property of multiplication always work?" or "Why is the product of two odd numbers always odd?" by testing a few cases—even strategically chosen cases—to use as the basis for their thinking.[4] Such empirical arguments are often convincing to children and, in fact, can be a useful way to begin to make sense of a problem situation that can lead to more general arguments. However, because empirical arguments show that a claim is true only in the specific cases tested, they lack the necessary generality reflected in more sophisticated justifications.

Rather than construct empirical arguments, children might instead build arguments based on the use of a representation—physical or pictorial—of the problem situation. Such representation-based arguments (Schifter 2009) can serve as a bridge between empirical arguments and formal arguments because children can reason with these *as if they represent an arbitrary case*.

In one third-grade classroom, students' thinking about whether or not the generalization "the sum of two even numbers is even" is true for any two even numbers illustrates children's capacity to build more general arguments. As Schifter (2009) reports, these children had already established that a number is even if the objects (e.g., cubes) representing the even number can be arranged in pairs with no objects left over. Similarly, a number is odd if, when the corresponding number of objects is arranged in pairs, there is one object left without a partner. Students gave the following arguments to support their claims:

Paul: I know the sum is even because my older sister told me it always happens that way.

Zoe: I know it will add to an even number because 4 + 4 = 8 and 8 + 8 = 16.

Juan:	Also, 6 + 12 = 18 and 32 + 20 = 52.
Eva:	We really can't know! Because we might not know about an even number, and if we add it with 2 it might equal an odd number!
James:	We can never know for sure, because the numbers don't stop.
Claudia:	We don't know because numbers don't end. One million plus one hundred. You can always add another hundred.
Melody:	Your answer will be even, because you are using even numbers.

As Melody spoke, she pointed to the arrangements of cubes in front of her.

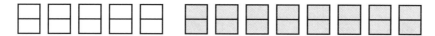

Then she continued:

Melody:	This number is in pairs (pointing to the light-colored cubes), and this number is in pairs (pointing to the dark-colored cubes), and when you put them together, it's still in pairs. (Schifter 2009, p. 73)

There are a variety of arguments used here. Paul's argument is based on an appeal to authority (Carpenter, Franke, and Levi 2003). Zoe offers an empirical argument based on adding an even number to itself, and Juan extends this by adding two different even numbers. Eva's response is critical. She suggests that the empirical arguments offered by Zoe and Juan are limited because there might be a situation, untested in the empirical cases, in which the claim is not true. James and Claudia reinforce this thinking by noting that there is an infinite number of even numbers, so they cannot test all the cases and, hence, "never know for sure." Melody then uses the cubes representing two specific even numbers (10 and 18) as if they represented two *general* even numbers in her argument; that is, her reasoning was not based on the fact that the numbers represented by the cubes were actually 10 and 18. Instead, she reasoned with the representations of 10 and 18 *as if they represented arbitrary numbers*. Her justification was based on the recognition that joining two representations of arbitrary numbers, neither of which had a single cube left over, would likewise result in a new representation without a single cube left over. In this sense, the representation became an important way for Melody to construct an argument more general than that of Zoe and James.

Mrs. Gardiner's third-grade students exhibited similar types of thinking when they explored whether the sum of two odd numbers would be even or odd. She asked them to think about the following question in small groups:

Task 3: Jesse's teacher gives him a new task. He has to add two odd numbers. Do you think his answer will be an even number or an odd number?

Students were given unifix cubes to use in their small-group work. After about 20 minutes of exploration, the following exchange occurred:

Teacher: I have been going around the room, and there are some wonderful things going on. Who would like to share their conjecture?

Luke: I think that when you add an odd to another odd number your sum will be even.

Teacher: Who agrees with Luke?

All groups except one raised their hand, agreeing with Luke.

Teacher: Group two, you don't agree with Luke?

Jenna: Well we thought it was true, but then we found a situation where it wasn't true.

Teacher: Okay, share that with us.

Jenna: Eight plus five equals thirteen.

Teacher: Okay, is eight an even number or an odd number?

Jenna: Oh! Oops! Okay, we agree with Lucas!

Teacher: Okay, since we all like Luke's conjecture, let me write it on the board. Now, who can explain *why* they think an odd plus an odd will always be even?

Jordan: Well, I did it with blocks, so I took nine blocks and I added it to eleven. If you look at the blocks alone, 9 and 11, then they each have a leftover, but when you put them together, their leftovers get paired up, so you have an even number.

(See fig. 4.2 for an illustration of Jordan's argument.)

The physical representation of two numbers—9 and 11—served as a springboard for Jordan's reasoning about what would happen if he added two arbitrary odd numbers. In essence, he seemed to use 9 and 11 as if they represented any two odd numbers. If he added any two odd numbers, each would have a one-cube leftover that, when paired or "added," would result in no leftovers. Hence, the sum would always be even.

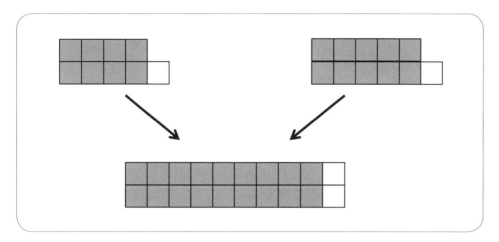

Figure 4.2. Jordan's representation

Another type of more general argument children can construct is one in which they reason with previously established generalizations as objects themselves. Like representation-based arguments, this type of reasoning is more sophisticated than empirical arguments because it does not depend on checking specific numerical cases (although children might use an example to illustrate a general principle). One fifth-grade teacher described the discussion in her classroom about the question "What if you had some odd numbers but didn't know how many there were? If you added them together, would your result be an even number or an odd number?"

Students reasoned that when two odd numbers are added, the result is even; when three odd numbers are added, the result is odd. From this, they extrapolated that the sum of four odd numbers would be even. As one student explained, "It is even because there are four [odd] numbers and that is an even amount of odd numbers." Reasoning inductively from generalizations about the sums of two, three, and four odd numbers, another student extended this idea, conjecturing that "When you add an odd amount of odd numbers, you will get an odd number; when you add an even amount of odd numbers, you will get an even number" (Blanton 2008, pp. 16–17). Students' reasoning did not involve checking cases, but appealing to generalizations they had already established in their classroom (e.g., "The sum of two odd numbers is even").

Relationships Between or Among Quantities

While justifying generalizations is often thought of with regard to arguments made to support general claims (such as "the product of any number of odd numbers will always be odd"), children can also be asked to justify the actions they make on objects, such as equations, involving generalized quantities. Kevin's justification of how he solved the equation $47 - y - y = 30 - y$ illustrates this:

> All of those y's represent the same amount. On one side, you are taking that amount away twice, and on the other side, only once. I am not going to think of taking one of those y's away on the left, and I am not going to think about taking the y away on the right. Since each side is having the same amount subtracted, I don't need to think about it. Then I just have $47 - y = 30$, so y is 17. (Blanton et al. 2011, p. 28)

Kevin's reasoning intuitively invokes the generalization that adding the same amount to equivalent quantities results in equivalent quantities. In a formal algebra course, this property leads to a procedure whereby students might formally add the same amount (y) to both sides of the equation and then simplify to obtain an equivalent form. It is important to note that Kevin does not formally apply this procedure. Instead, he notices that within the structural form of the equation there are equivalent objects on both sides (y), so he can, in effect, ignore these parts because "each side is having the same amount subtracted" and reason with an easier, equivalent equation: $47 - y = 30$. The goal of early algebra is not to teach children to use formal procedures but instead to help them bring their emergent understandings of the equals sign, operations, and generalized quantities (e.g., the quantities $47 - y - y$ and $30 - y$) to bear in reasoning about relationships between these quantities, much like Kevin does here.

Functional Thinking

The nature of the arguments that children build to justify generalizations about functional relationships is often empirical at first but can evolve into more general forms based on the problem context. For example, to reason that their relationship or rule is correct, children might initially test the cases identified in a function table. With Growing Train and a rule such as $R + R = V$, they might substitute values in the rule to check that $1 + 1 = 2$, $3 + 3 = 6$, and so on. This argument is a bit circular, however, in that the general rule was derived from the numerical cases in the table.

Instead, children can sometimes reason more generally from the problem context to justify the nature of the rule. The Trapezoid Tables problem, where people are seated at trapezoid-shaped tables joined end-to-end (see fig. 4.3 for one-table and two-table configurations), illustrates this thinking.

Figure 4.3. Trapezoid tables

Children in Mrs. Soares' third-grade classroom were asked to find a relationship between the number of tables and the number of people who could be seated at the tables for any number of tables. They came up with the rule $P = 3(t) + 2$, where P represented the number of people and t the number of tables. They reasoned that their rule was correct by noting that, in the problem context, there would always be 2 people seated on the ends (denoted by + 2 in the rule) and that each trapezoid table always had a total of 3 people who could sit "on the top and the bottom." The total number of people on the top and bottom, then, varied by the number of tables and could be represented as $3 \times t$ (Blanton 2008).

Justifying a function rule in this way requires children to make sense of the attributes of a problem (e.g., that two people always sit on the end, regardless of the number of tables) and how these attributes can be modeled mathematically. Their reasoning is algebraic in nature because it requires them to think about generalized quantities and how they are connected to and can be represented by the problem situation.

Connections to Curricular Standards

The importance of justifying one's mathematical thinking and evaluating the arguments of others is clearly set forth in current standards (NGA Center and CCSSO 2010; NCTM 2000). The *Common Core State Standards for Mathematics* captures this in the practice "Construct viable arguments and critique the reasoning of others" (SMP 3). This type of thinking was evident when Eva and James called into question the empirical argument made by Zoe and Juan. Moreover, this standard states that mathematically proficient students should "reason inductively about data, making plausible arguments that take into account the context from which the data arose" (SMP 3e). This proficiency was illustrated by Mrs. Soares' children, who were able to justify their function rule by reasoning about the arrangements of people seated at trapezoid-shaped tables. Elementary students, in particular, should be able to "construct arguments using concrete referents such as objects, drawings, diagrams, and actions" (SMP 3g), as Melody and Jordan did in their representation-based arguments about sums of evens and odds.

The foregoing examples reflect core aspects of algebraic reasoning as a practice of justifying generalizations. To express this another way, children are *reasoning algebraically* when they evaluate others' justifications of generalized claims, as Eva and James did with Zoe and Juan's arguments. They are *reasoning algebraically* when they use the problem context as an additional basis for justifying their claims, as Mrs. Soares's third graders did when justifying a relationship between the number of trapezoid-shaped tables and the number of people who could be seated at the tables. They are *reasoning algebraically* when they construct representation-based arguments to justify arithmetic generalizations, as Melody and Jordan did in their arguments about sums of evens and odds. Although the sophistication of children's arguments will vary as their reasoning matures, the characteristic of their reasoning that makes it algebraic is when they construct or evaluate arguments that deal with generalized claims, not claims about particular instances.

Algebraic Reasoning as a Practice of Acting on Generalizations

Perhaps the most complex of the four practices of algebraic reasoning is *acting on generalizations*—or reasoning with generalizations—as objects themselves. While all four practices reflect algebraic reasoning, reasoning as acting on a generalization is unique in that it entails reasoning with a generalization as an object in and of itself; that is, once children have noticed, represented, and justified a mathematical generalization—all of which are processes of algebraic reasoning—it is important that they be able to apply this generalization in reasoning about problems.

Generalized Arithmetic

Reasoning as acting on generalizations can begin in the simple computational work that children do in the study of arithmetic. For example, when children use key arithmetic relationships such as the fundamental properties to solve arithmetic problems, they are using important relational thinking strategies that are characteristic of algebraic reasoning (Carpenter, Franke, and Levi 2003; Empson and Levi 2011). As Blanton et al. (2011) describe it, algebraic understanding includes not only that children see these properties as generalizations that apply to all numbers but also that they be able to "represent them symbolically and *identify their use explicitly in computations* [emphasis added] (p. 18)." They note that reasoning algebraically with the fundamental properties can begin at an informal, intuitive level when children invoke a property in solving arithmetic problems, even before they are explicitly aware that they are doing so or why. Elena's reasoning in the following problem illustrates such a situation:

Task 4: Martinique has 6 boxes of marbles, with 23 marbles in each box. How many marbles does Martinique have altogether?

"Elena reasoned, 'I will do the 20s and then the 3s. Six groups of 20 are 120; 6 groups of 3 are 18. There would be 120 plus 18, or 138 marbles'" (Blanton et al. 2011, p. 17).

At this point, Elena is informally applying the distributive property of multiplication over addition; that is, she is able to invoke the property without being able to explicitly recognize it or its use.

If we treat this type of reasoning as a starting point, arithmetic then provides an opportunity for children's reasoning with the fundamental properties to advance, so that they come to recognize a property as an object in their computational work and can explicitly identify it as the justification for their arithmetic moves. Simple computational strings, such as the following, provide such an opportunity.

$$563 \times 0 + 341 + 273 - 273$$

Children who cannot reason algebraically would likely use standard algorithms and perform the indicated operations in a linear, left-to-right fashion. They might multiply 563 and 0, add 341, then add 273, and, finally, subtract 273. While this will produce a correct result, it does not tap into the rich relationships captured by the fundamental properties. Instead, children are reasoning algebraically when they can process the entire string holistically, invoke fundamental properties to compute more efficiently, and, ultimately, identify the use of these properties in their computational work. As one fourth grader, Lilly, reasoned, "Any number times 0 is just 0, so 563×0 is 0. And any number subtracted from itself is 0, so $273 - 273$ is 0. That leaves 341 as the answer." With this type of reasoning, Lilly did not need to actually compute but could invoke and identify generalizations as objects in her reasoning.

As we saw in the previous section on justifying generalizations, in the particular case where children use previously established generalizations as the basis for their argument that a new generalization is true (or false), their practice of justifying might itself be described as acting on a generalization. For example, a second grade student used the generalizations $b - b = 0$ and $a + 0 = a$ to reason that $a + b - b = a$ is true (Carpenter, Franke, and Levi 2003). In this case the student is acting on two generalizations as objects themselves in order to reason about the truth of a new claim. Similarly, using previously established generalizations about sums or products of even numbers and odd numbers to justify a new claim entails reasoning with a generalization as an object itself.

Relationships Between or Among Quantities

As described earlier, children are reasoning algebraically when they think structurally, or relationally, about how two quantities are related. For example, children who find the missing value in an equation such as $10 \times 4 = \underline{\hspace{1cm}} \times 8$ or even in $10 \times 4 = t \times 8$ by reasoning that since 8 is 2 times 4, then the missing value must be $^{1}/_{2}$ of 10, are reasoning algebraically about the structural relationship between two quantities (10×4 and $t \times 8$). Children who think operationally about the equals sign will typically claim—incorrectly—that the missing number is 40 (10×4), or even 320 ($10 \times 4 \times 8$). In the third-grade classroom described earlier (p. 78) in which the lesson focused on the meaning of the equals sign, students explored whether equations were true or false and reasoned about what values would make an open equation true (Carpenter, Franke, and Levi 2003). Using Robert's view of the equals sign (p. 78), students gave the following arguments for why 3 might be the unknown value in the equation $4 + 7 = \underline{\hspace{1cm}} + 8$:

Dan: Well, when you have $4 + 7$, it equals 11, so like um, when you have 8 and you add 3 to it, it's 11.

Nolan: Well, I said if $7 + 4$ equals 11, then $8 + 3$ must equal 11, too, because 8 is a greater number than 7 so for $7 + 4$ you would have to put 4 there because it's not as great as 8. For 8 you'd have to put a 3 because [8 is] one greater than 7 and 4 is 1 greater than 3.

While these strategies are different (Dan's was computational in nature, whereas Nolan's *compensation* strategy relied on thinking about relationships among the numbers), both reflect important ways of reasoning relationally about the equals sign to find the unknown value.

Learning to see equations (and inequalities) structurally in terms of the quantitative relationships they depict—in the way that Nolan reasoned about the unknown value in $4 + 7 = \underline{\hspace{1cm}} + 8$—is an important prerequisite for operating on generalized quantities to solve equations. The equation $5(n + 2) = 20$ illustrates this point as well. In formal algebra, students might learn procedural rules for solving equations by which they first divide both sides of this equation by 5 (or multiply both sides by the inverse of 5) to produce the equivalent equation $n + 2 = 4$ and then subtract 2 from both sides of the equation to determine that $n = 2$. Although this process is correct, if children learn to see the structural relationship between quantities such as $5(n + 2)$ and 20, they can act on these (generalized) quantities as objects themselves in order to solve equations more efficiently in much the same way they might see relationships within a computational string that allows them to compute more efficiently. For example, they might notice that, since 5 times a quantity ($n + 2$) is equivalent to 20, then that quantity must be equivalent to 4, since $5 \times 4 = 20$. From this, they can reason that $n + 2$ must be equivalent to 4, so $n = 2$.

One third-grade teacher described how her student, Sam, reasoned about the equation $(3 \times n) + 2 = 14$:

> Sam said that we could take the 2 away. He said that if we take the 2 from one side we have to take it from the other side as well. This was to make it balance. After we [took] the 2 away, he said to take the 12 tiles and put them in groups of 3. There were 4 groups, so the answer had to be 4. We tried replacing the n with 4, and it worked (Blanton and Kaput 2005, p. 422).

Rather than apply a formal procedure (and likely a meaningless one for a third grader) for solving an equation, Sam reasoned that the generalized quantity $3 \times n$ had to be equivalent to 12 because he understood the equals sign as representing a relationship of equivalence. Applying his understanding of multiplication by arranging the 12 tiles in groups of 3, he was able to determine—without doing procedural algebraic manipulations—that the value of n had to be 4.

As Dougherty (2010) describes, representing comparisons between two quantities symbolically enables children to act on these quantities without manipulating physical referents for them. In turn, this can prepare these students to act on generalized quantities in equivalent and inequality relationships in a more formal study of algebra in later grades. In the Piggy Bank problem (p. 71), children are reasoning algebraically when they act on the generalized quantities that represent the number of pennies Tim and Angela each have and represent the relationship between these quantities as, say, $P < P + 8$ without the need to manipulate physical referents such as pennies in a bank.

Functional Thinking

Children can use the functional relationships they develop, whether it be in words, variable notation, or coordinate graphs, as objects in their reasoning. For example, Blanton, Brizuela, and colleagues (2015) report that in Growing Train Rebecca generalized a relationship which she represented with variable notation as $R + R = V$, with R representing the number of train stops and V representing the total number of cars after R stops. When Rebecca was asked, "If we also count the engine, how would this affect the values in your table? How would this affect your rule?" (p. 73), she explained that she would just "add one more" to the table values for the number of cars. But even more important, she was able to reason algebraically from her original function rule and represent the new relationship for which the engine is counted as $1 + R + R = V$. In other words, the symbolic rule $R + R = V$ was in her thinking an object that she could manipulate in order to model a new problem situation. She did not need to construct a new function table for the revised problem and reason inductively from it (as she had with the original task) in order to generalize the new relationship.

Coordinate graphs are a useful way to represent functional relationships, and acting on these graphical representations is an important form of algebraic reasoning. Research shows that children not only can construct coordinate graphs to represent generalized relationships between two quantities, but they also can begin to reason with both qualitative and quantitative graphical representations of functional relationships as objects in their thinking (Brizuela and Earnest 2008). For example, Tierney and Monk (2008) discuss how qualitative graphs served as tools with which fourth-grade students reasoned by using graphs as objects that depicted relationships between varying quantities. The absence of quantifying information, such as scales or procedural calculations, in a graph that compared the growth of two types of plants (see fig. 4.4) pushed children to focus on general meanings depicted in the shapes of the graphs as these shapes related to the rates of the plants' growth rather than on specific points of interest.

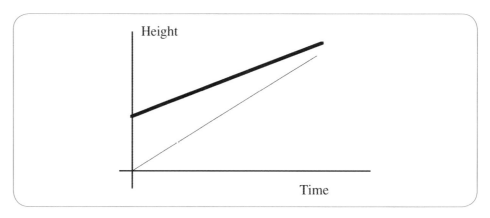

Fig. 4.4. Graphs representing the growth of fast plants

Acting on generalizations as a form of algebraic reasoning enables children to build on and exploit previously established understandings in ways that extend and deepen their algebra knowledge. As the study of algebra—particularly within the context of functions—becomes more formalized in middle grades and high school, students will be expected to reason fluently with different representations—graphs, variable notation, tables—in order to explain and predict function behavior. When children are given opportunities to act on generalizations as Rebecca did, their algebraic reasoning improves and prepares them for more advanced mathematical thinking in later grades.

Connections to Curricular Standards

When children reason algebraically by acting on generalizations as objects, they are engaged in the practice of "making use of structure" (SMP 7). Lilly exhibited this kind of thinking when she used fundamental properties to reason about a computational string. For example, she was able to make use of the structure characterized by the additive inverse property by noticing its occurrence in a computational string and by invoking it—making use of it—to compute efficiently rather than relying on a computational algorithm. In other words, she was able to "see complicated things, such as algebraic expressions, as single objects or as being composed of several objects" (SMP 7d; NGA Center and CCSSO 2010, p. 8). We see the same thinking at work in Sam's reasoning about the solution to the equation $(3 \times n) + 2 = 14$ as well as in Rebecca's use of the functional relationship $R + R = V$ to represent new information about counting the train engine. Blanton et al. (2011) also point out that this type of thinking is critical in preparing students for the study of algebra in secondary grades because the transformational aspects of algebra, that is, processes such as simplifying expressions and solving equations and inequalities, studied in these grades require students to see expressions and equations as objects rather than a series of computations.

Connections to Classroom Practice

The most important classroom objectives for teachers in developing children's algebraic reasoning is to encourage children to look for, represent, and justify generalizations, and to reason with these as objects in their thinking. As this chapter highlights, these practices can develop in a number of different ways. This might include having children explore the structure of the fundamental properties that governs how operations behave, arithmetic relationships in classes of numbers, relationships among generalized quantities, or functional relationships between two covarying quantities.

In planning mathematics lessons, teachers should consider whether the mathematical content being used affords children opportunities to think about general mathematical structure or relationships; that is, are there regular opportunities for students to think beyond particular numbers and notice, represent, and reason with any underlying structure or general claims? If there are none, then it is important to consider how lesson tasks can be nuanced to elicit children's algebraic reasoning. Tasks that fall short of this important mathematical work ultimately do not have the sufficient depth for engaging children in the kinds of thinking that will prepare them for the study of more formal mathematics—particularly algebra—in later grades.

As this chapter suggests, there are practical ways to sharpen the algebraic focus in classroom instruction. Computational work can be a simple starting point (Blanton et al. 2011). To begin with, teachers can choose numbers in computational tasks that help children notice underlying structure such as the fundamental properties. For example, if children are learning how to multiply two-digit numbers, computational tasks can be designed so that children might observe the commutative property of multiplication or the multiplicative identity property. Finding the products 34×15 and 15×34, rather than, say, 34×15 and 27×18, can set up a deeper discussion about the behavior of the operation $\times$ when the order of the factors is reversed.

Tasks should be designed to help children confront misconceptions about the generalizations they form. As children operate on numbers, they sometimes develop generalizations that are not true for a given domain. For example, children might conclude that "multiplying any two numbers always results in a larger number." Such misconceptions are often a natural result of operations on numbers in only certain number domains (e.g., the counting numbers). While such domains are chosen because they are familiar to students, their use can unintentionally promote misconceptions in children's thinking. However, these types of misconceptions afford students a rich opportunity for learning to recognize and use counterexamples as they reason about generalized claims (SMP 3d). For example, asking children to think about the product of two numbers, where at least one is not a counting number, can help them identify counterexamples to the claim that "multiplying any two numbers always results in a larger number."

Computational tasks should include those that are designed in ways that children cannot—or are not allowed to—use an algorithm. Moreover, children should be asked to justify the mathematical moves they use in their computational work. For example, a computational string such as $(289 + 345) \times 0 + 45 - 45$ provides children with a simple context in which they might apply and identify the properties in use. A child who understands that any number multiplied by zero is equal to zero and that any number subtracted from itself is equal to zero can quickly and efficiently invoke this understanding to determine that $(289 + 345) \times 0 + 45 - 45 = 0$. Without a rich understanding of these properties, children will be limited to algorithmic thinking and will proceed in a left-to-right manner, performing the computations as they occur.

Computational tasks should be written in formats other than standard format. For example, simple tasks like $3 \times 5 =$___ are often used in arithmetic-focused curricula, but they prompt children to think that the symbol = acts like an operator, or a call to perform the indicated operation. It is important that children see equations—whether they involve only numerical values or generalized quantities—in nonstandard formats. To this end, tasks like $5 + 7 =$ ___ $+ 6$ offer simple ways to quickly assess misconceptions in children's understanding of the equals sign.

Tasks should be designed to help children decompose quantities in insightful ways. For example, 50×103 can be decomposed using the distributive property of multiplication over addition and computed more efficiently if it is seen as equivalent to $50 \times (100 + 3)$ and, subsequently, as equivalent to $(50 \times 100) + (50 \times 3)$. While children might not explicitly write these equivalent forms when performing this computation, those with a rich understanding of relationships in numbers will be able to use the underlying structure of the number system to flexibly decompose—as well as compose—quantities in such a way. Simple tasks for which children are asked to think about *how* they might *best* compute—rather than just apply an algorithm without thought—can develop their algebraic reasoning. As Blanton et al. (2011) describe, "[E]xperiences in decomposing quantities help build a foundation for simplifying algebraic expressions in the middle grades and high school because they can be used to focus attention on the structure of quantities and how they are composed (and hence, decomposed) and how the fundamental properties are used to compose and decompose quantities (p. 73)."

Finally, many arithmetic tasks can be modified in subtle ways to extend arithmetic work to algebraic thinking (Carraher et al. 2008). For example, children are often asked to solve word problems with two known quantities to find a numerical solution, such as in the following task:

> **Task 5:** *Charlotte decorates 3 cupcakes each day for 5 days. How many cupcakes does she decorate in all?*

Simply making one of the known quantities an unknown quantity changes this arithmetic problem to one that requires algebraic reasoning:

> **Task 6:** *Charlotte decorates the same number of cupcakes each day for 5 days. How would you represent the number of cupcakes she decorates all together?*

In this revised task, children need to understand that the number of cupcakes is an unknown quantity whose value—in the absence of more information—can vary. They need to be able to represent the unknown number of cupcakes decorated on a given day as a generalized quantity in order to represent the total number of cupcakes decorated over 5 days.

Another similar approach is to vary a task parameter so that an arithmetic task becomes a functional thinking task (Blanton 2008). Again, the cupcake problem can be revised to illustrate this principle:

Task 7: *If Charlotte decorates 3 cupcakes each day, how many cupcakes does she decorate all together for two days? Three days? Four days? N days? Find a relationship between the number of days and the total number of cupcakes she decorates.*

Here, students are asked to think beyond the particular instance of 3 cupcakes each day for 5 days and to think instead about a functional relationship between the number of days and the number of decorated cupcakes.

Finally, teachers can extend tasks so that students use the generalizations they develop in their reasoning. The power of this practice, of acting on generalizations as objects, is that it helps children build on their existing knowledge to create new understandings. For example, if children recognize that the sum of an even number and an odd number is always odd and that the sum of two odd numbers is always even, then they can use these generalizations to examine the sum of three odd numbers without reverting to checking numerical cases.

Simple variations like these on the arithmetic content addressed in instruction can deepen and extend children's algebraic reasoning and help children see mathematical ideas with more depth and coherence than a superficial treatment of arithmetic could. However, the manner in which tasks are implemented in instruction is just as important as the tasks themselves. As children look for mathematical generalizations, they should be encouraged to represent their generalizations in different ways, to describe the meanings of their representations, and to explain how two different representations might be connected. Classroom practice should promote vigorous debate about children's general claims and the strength—or generality—of the arguments they make to support these claims. Children should be expected to think about both *why* and *when* their claims are true. As Mrs. Gardiner's class explored generalizations about even numbers and odd numbers, she encouraged them to think about whether their generalizations would always be true *and* why this might be the case. This practice can help children develop an appreciation that mathematical thinkers critically examine whether or not claims are true and continually look for confirming or disconfirming evidence. As illustrated in the discussion among Melody and her classmates (Schifter 2009), collective reasoning is a powerful mechanism for developing viable arguments if children are encouraged to thoughtfully examine each other's claims. Students should be expected to evaluate the strength of their arguments, to look for weaknesses, and to understand whether their arguments are sufficiently general.

Conclusion

The goal of this chapter has been to examine what algebraic reasoning looks like in grades 3–5 classrooms. *Algebraic* reasoning is distinguished here from other forms of reasoning because of its focus on the practices of generalizing, representing, justifying, and reasoning with mathematical structure and relationships. While other forms of reasoning might entail representing or justifying one's thinking, or even acting on these representations, the critical distinction between these forms and algebraic reasoning is that algebraic reasoning entails reasoning with generalized quantities or generalizations.

It is equally important to understand what early algebra—and algebraic reasoning—is not. As described elsewhere (Carraher et al. 2008), early algebra is *not* "algebra early"; that is, while early algebra contains many of the elements of formal algebra—for example, algebraic equations and expressions, graphs, tables, functions—it is not intended to be treated as formal algebra repackaged for young children. It does not focus on teaching procedures for the transformational aspects of algebra—such as solving equations or simplifying expressions—that have often characterized traditional high school algebra instruction. It does not intend to use algebraic artifacts—such as variable notation—without meaning or context or in ways that children have not produced through their own investigations. Instead, as this chapter alludes, early algebra draws on different points of entry that include arithmetic, functional thinking, mathematical modeling, and quantitative reasoning (Carraher and Schliemann 2007). It then uses these points of entry for children to engage in the practices of generalizing, representing and justifying generalized claims, and reasoning with the generalizations they produce as objects themselves. The essence of this work is reasoning and sense making.

Before the inception of early algebra, the school mathematics curriculum was based on an "arithmetic-then-algebra" approach, where it was presumed that children must first learn arithmetic before they study algebra. This approach led to significant student failure rates in high school algebra courses that marginalized students in school and ultimately "gate-kept" them from a wide array of careers in technical fields (Kaput 2008; Kilpatrick, Swafford, and Findell 2001; Schoenfeld 1995). More important, this approach is counterintuitive to a fundamental assumption of early algebra: Children will not learn arithmetic well apart from generalizing, representing, justifying, and reasoning with the structure and relationships implicit in it. From this perspective, early algebra is critical not only because it will prepare children for a study of mathematics in later grades but also because it will help them more deeply understand the mathematical—arithmetic—content they learn in the elementary grades.

NCTM's *Principles and Standards for School Mathematics* (2000) and, more recently, the *Common Core State Standards* (2010) have set forth an ambitious agenda for developing mathematically proficient students across school mathematics. Algebraic reasoning is a central part of this agenda, beginning as early as prekindergarten. Building on NCTM's Process Standards, the *Common Core's* Standards for Mathematical Practice help to further define the notion of mathematically proficient students. As noted earlier, if we extract core ideas from these practices, we might summarize them as: (1) noticing regularity or structure (SMP 7, 8), (2) expressing regularity and structure with precision (SMP 6), (3) constructing appropriate arguments (SMP 3), (4) making use of and reasoning with structure (SMP 2, 7), and (5) solving problems by modeling situations and using appropriate tools strategically (SMP 4, 5). As this chapter details, items 1 to 4 are deeply connected to the four key practices of algebraic thinking discussed here. Item 5, too, reflects fundamental characteristics of good algebraic reasoning tasks whereby children are asked to investigate problem situations, model or represent mathematical relationships and structure, and use appropriate tools— words, tables, graphs, pictures, and variable notation—to facilitate their thinking. This synergy not only underscores the power of early algebra as a way to develop *Common Core*'s Standards for Mathematical Practice in children's thinking, it also elevates early algebra as a forward-looking approach to teaching and learning mathematics in the elementary grades. In the end, children will be the ones who benefit.

Notes

1. Hereafter referred to as the fundamental properties, these include important properties such as the additive identity, the additive inverse, the commutative property of addition, the commutative property of multiplication, and the distributive property of multiplication over addition. See Blanton et al. (2011) for a complete list.

2. Although Rebecca was a first grader, her thinking—and this type of task—is similar to what we should see in grades 3–5. All names are pseudonyms.

3. Because "proof" has a specific meaning in formal mathematics, the less formal terms "justification" and "argument" are used in this chapter.

4. Fundamental properties, such as the commutative property of multiplication, are axioms that are assumed to be true without proof. However, children need to be convinced— and to convince others—that these types of generalizations are reasonable in that they accurately capture predictable behaviors of operations.

References

Blanton, M. *Algebra in Elementary Classrooms: Transforming Thinking, Transforming Practice.* Portsmouth, N.H.: Heinemann, 2008.

Blanton, M. L., B. M. Brizuela, A. Gardiner, K. Sawrey, and A. Newman-Owens. "A Learning Trajectory in Six-year-olds' Thinking About Generalizing Functional Relationships." *Journal for Research in Mathematics Education* 46, no. 5 (2015): 511–558.

Blanton, M., and J. Kaput. "Design Principles for Instructional Contexts That Support Students' Transition from Arithmetic to Algebraic Reasoning: Elements of Task and Culture." In *Everyday Matters in Science and Mathematics,* edited by R. Nemirovsky, B. Warren, A. Rosebery, and J. Solomon, pp. 211–234. Mahwah, N.J.: Lawrence Erlbaum, 2004.

Blanton, M., and J. Kaput. "Characterizing a Classroom Practice That Promotes Algebraic Reasoning." *Journal for Research in Mathematics Education* 36, no. 5 (2005): 412–446.

Blanton, M., L. Levi, T. Crites, and B. Dougherty. *Developing Essential Understanding of Algebraic Thinking for Teaching Mathematics in Grades 3–5* (Essential Understanding Series). Reston, Va.: National Council of Teachers of Mathematics, 2011.

Blanton, M., A. Stephens, E. Knuth, A. Gardiner, I. Isler, and J. Kim. "The Development of Children's Algebraic Thinking: The Impact of a Comprehensive Early Algebra Intervention in Third Grade." *Journal for Research in Mathematics Education* 46, no. 1 (2015): 39–87.

Brizuela, B. M., and M. Alvarado. "First Graders' Work on Additive Problems with the Use of Different Notational Tools." *Revista IRICE Nueva* Época 21 (2010): 37–44.

Brizuela, B. M., M. Blanton, A. Gardiner, K. Sawrey, K. Yangsook, and A. Gibbons. "First Graders' Use of Variable Notation in a Teaching Experiment." Paper presented at the NCTM Research Conference, San Francisco, CA, 2016.

Brizuela, B. M., M. Blanton, K. Sawrey, A. Newman-Owens, and A. Gardiner. "Children's Use of Variables and Variable Notation to Represent Their Algebraic Ideas." *Mathematical Thinking and Learning* 17 no. 1 (2015): 34–63.

Brizuela, B. M., and D. Earnest. "Multiple Notational Systems and Algebraic Understandings: The Case of the "Best Deal" Problem. In *Algebra in the Early Grades,* edited by J. Kaput, D. Carraher, and M. Blanton, pp. 273–301. Mahwah, N.J.: Lawrence Erlbaum & Associates, 2008.

Brizuela, B. M., and S. Lara-Roth. "Additive Relations and Function Tables." *Journal of Mathematical Behavior,* 20 no. 3 (2002): 309–319.

Cai, J., S. F. Ng, and J. C. Moyer. "Developing Students' Algebraic Thinking in Earlier Grades: Lessons from China and Singapore." In *Advances in Mathematics Education Monograph Series,* edited by J. Cai and E. Knuth, pp. 25–41, Early Algebraization: A Global Dialogue from Multiple Perspectives. New York: Springer, 2011.

Carpenter, T. P., M. Franke, and L. Levi. *Thinking Mathematically: Integrating Arithmetic and Algebra in Elementary School.* Portsmouth, N.H.: Heinemann, 2003.

Carraher, D., and A. Schliemann. "Early Algebra." In *Second Handbook of Research on Mathematics Teaching and Learning,* edited by F. K. Lester, pp. 669–705. Charlotte, N.C.: Information Age, 2007.

Carraher, D. W., A. D. Schliemann, B. M. Brizuela, and D. Earnest. "Arithmetic and Algebra in Early Mathematics Education. *Journal for Research in Mathematics Education* 37, no. 2 (2006): 87–115.

Carraher, D., A. D. Schliemann, and J. Schwartz. "Early Algebra Is Not the Same as Algebra Early." In *Algebra in the Early Grades*, edited by J. Kaput, D. Carraher, and M. Blanton, pp. 235–272. Mahwah, N.J.: Lawrence Erlbaum & Associates/Taylor & Francis Group, 2008.

Common Core State Standards Initiative (CCSSI). *Common Core State Standards for Mathematics.* Washington, D.C.: National Governors Association Center for Best Practices and the Council of Chief State School Officers, 2010. http://www.corestandards.org/wp-content /uploads/Math_Standards.pdf

Dougherty, B. (2008). "Measure Up: A Quantitative View of Early Algebra." In *Algebra in the Early Grades,* edited by J. Kaput, D. Carraher, and M. Blanton, pp. 389–412. New York: Lawrence Erlbaum & Associates, 2008.

Dougherty, B. "A Davydov Approach to Early Mathematics." In *Future Curricular Trends in Algebra and Geometry,* edited by Z. Usiskin, K. Andersen, and N. Zotto, pp. 63–69. Charlotte, N.C.: Information Age Publishing, 2010.

Empson, S. B., and L. Levi. *Extending Children's Mathematics: Fractions and Decimals.* Portsmouth, N.H.: Heinemann, 2011.

Kaput, J. "Transforming Algebra from an Engine of Inequity to an Engine of Mathematical Power by 'Algebrafying' the K–12 Curriculum. In *The Nature and Role of Algebra in the K–14 Curriculum: Proceedings of a National Symposium,* edited by the National Council of Teachers of Mathematics and Mathematical Sciences Education Board, pp. 25–26. Washington, D.C.: National Academy Press, 1998.

Kaput, J. "What Is Algebra? What Is Algebraic Reasoning?" In *Algebra in the Early Grades,* edited by J. Kaput, D. Carraher, and M. Blanton, pp. 5–17. Mahwah, N.J.: Lawrence Erlbaum & Associates/Taylor & Francis Group, 2008.

Kilpatrick, J., J. Swafford, and B. Findell. *Adding It Up: Helping Children Learn Mathematics.* Washington, D.C.: National Academy Press, 2011.

Knuth, E. J., M. W. Alibali, N. M. McNeil, A. Weinberg, and A. C. Stephens. "Middle School Students' Understanding of Core Algebraic Concepts: Equality and Variable." *International Reviews on Mathematical Education* 37 (2005): 1–9.

Morris, A. K. "Representations That Enable Children to Engage in Deductive Arguments. In *Teaching and Learning Proof Across the Grades: A K–16 Perspective,* edited by D. Stylianou, M. Blanton, and E. Knuth, pp. 87–101. Mahwah, N.J.: Taylor & Francis Group, 2009.

National Council of Teachers of Mathematics (NCTM). *Curriculum and Evaluation Standards for School Mathematics.* Reston, Va.: National Council of Teachers of Mathematics, 1989.

National Council of Teachers of Mathematics. *Principles and Standards for School Mathematics.* Reston, Va.: NCTM, 2000.

National Council of Teachers of Mathematics. *Focus in High School Mathematics: Reasoning and Sense Making.* Reston, Va.: NCTM, 2009.

Schifter, D. "Representation-based Proof in the Elementary Grades. In *Teaching and Learning Proof Across the Grades: A K–16 Perspective,* edited by D. Stylianou, M. Blanton, and E. Knuth, pp. 71–86. Mahwah, N.J.: Taylor & Francis Group, 2009.

Schliemann, A. D., D. W. Carraher, and B. M. Brizuela. *Bringing Out the Algebraic Character of Arithmetic: From Children's Ideas to Classroom Practice.* Mahwah, N.J.: Lawrence Erlbaum & Associates, 2007.

Schoenfeld, A. H. "Is Thinking About 'Algebra' a Misdirection?" In *The Algebra Colloquium,* edited by C. Lacampagne, W. Blair, and J. Kaput, pp. 83–86, vol. 2, Working Group Papers. Washington, D.C.: U.S. Department of Education, Office of Educational Research and Improvement, 1995.

Tierney, C., and S. Monk. "Children's Reasoning About Change Over Time." In *Algebra in the Early Grades*, edited by J. Kaput, D. Carraher, and M. Blanton, pp. 185–200. Mahwah, N.J.: Lawrence Erlbaum & Associates, 2008.

Understanding and Developing Intermediate Students' Reasoning and Sense Making in Decomposing Shapes to Reason About Area and Volume Measurement[1]

Michael T. Battista

Katy, a second grader, was shown how a plastic inch-square fit in the upper-left indicated square on the 7-by-3–inch rectangle displayed in figure 5.1a. She was then asked, "How many plastic squares just like this would it take to completely cover the rectangle?" Katy drew and counted 30 squares, as shown in figure 5.1b (Battista 1999).

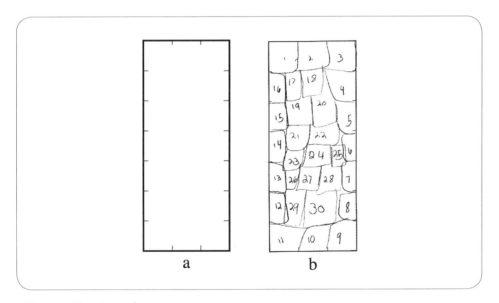

Fig. 5.1. Katy's work

Katy was then asked to predict how many plastic squares were needed to cover the rectangle shown in figure 5.2a. Without drawing, Katy pointed and counted as in figure 5.2b, predicting 30. When checking her answer with plastic squares, she pointed to and counted as shown in figure 5.2c, getting 30. When she counted the squares again, first she got 24, then 27.

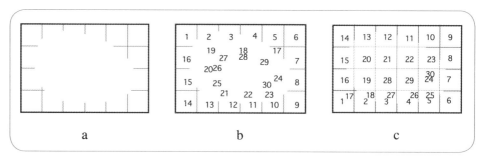

Fig. 5.2

Katy was not using row-by-column organizational reasoning to locate squares in these rectangular arrays. Although educated adults instantly "see" the squares arranged by rows and columns, Katy had not yet mentally constructed this organizing structure in her drawings or counting, even when she used physical materials.

Katy's difficulty is not unusual. When the problem in figure 5.1a was given to above-average students in grades 2–5, only 19 percent of second graders, 31 percent of third graders, 54 percent of fourth graders, and 78 percent of fifth graders made correct predictions (Battista 1996).[2] Clearly, early mathematics instruction is not properly enabling students to become proficient reasoners about decomposing shapes into organized sets of unit-squares in ways that are essential for measuring area.

In this chapter, we examine how middle-grade students make sense of and reason about the general topic of decomposing shapes, a critically important topic in geometry and geometric measurement.[3] We focus on geometric decomposition because almost all of the Common Core State Standards for Mathematics (CCSSM) geometry and geometric measurement standards for kindergarten–grade 8 involve decomposition in some way. Moreover, geometric decomposition is also important because it involves spatial visualization, which is the process of creating and manipulating mental images so that we can analyze, make sense of, and reason about spatial objects and actions even when they are not visible. As *Principles and Standards for School Mathematics* (*Principles and Standards*) states, "Spatial visualization—building and manipulating mental representations of two- and three-dimensional objects and perceiving an object from different perspectives—is an important aspect of geometric thinking" (NCTM 2000, p. 41). Almost all geometric reasoning, sense making, and problem solving is intimately connected to spatial visualization. Furthermore, the National Research Council claims that, "Underpinning success in mathematics and science is the capacity to think spatially" (NRC 2006, p. 6), a statement backed by much research (Newcombe 2010; Wai et al. 2009). And, because focusing on spatial reasoning in mathematics can improve the attitudes and self-confidence of low-achieving middle-school students (Wheatley and Wheatley 1979), such a focus can make mathematics accessible to more students. Indeed, one of the primary ways that we make sense of things is to visualize them in thought or action (SMP 1). Visualization enables us to reason about geometric *representations* such as physical objects, pictures/diagrams, and computer animations (SMP 1f, 1i, 2d, 3d, 6c; PS 5). So problem solving that involves spatial reasoning provides a powerful instructional context for developing *all* students' overall mathematical reasoning and sense making.

In this chapter, we examine how students make sense of geometric ideas in instructional contexts that support the *Principles and Standards* process of "building new mathematical knowledge through problem solving." In such contexts, students construct new knowledge by making, testing, and refining conjectures to eventually arrive at solutions that make intuitive sense to them. To teach in ways that support students' sense making and reasoning in such contexts, it is critical to recognize that most students do not make sense of mathematical ideas immediately. They go through numerous cycles of formulating, testing, and reflecting on their ideas. To support students' success in these learning cycles, teachers must give students problems that are conceptually accessible to them. Students must have opportunities to productively struggle with the problems and be given appropriate instructional monitoring and adjustment when the struggle becomes too demanding or frustrating. They must have opportunities to solidify their ideas by thoughtfully solving similar problems not by engaging in endless, mindless practice. They must have opportunities to generalize their ideas by applying them in new contexts and by using them to solve more complicated problems. They must be sufficiently supported when they are working in new contexts, because applying new concepts before they are completely solidified can overload students' reasoning capacity and thereby cause temporary setbacks in reasoning.

Processes and Practices in Geometric Reasoning and Sense Making

To fully support students' development of pre-proof geometric reasoning and sense making in teaching, it is important to understand the underlying core mental processes that they require. The four mental processes described below form the cognitive foundation on which the CCSSM Standards for Mathematical Practices (SMP) and NCTM Process Standards (PS)[4] in geometry are built. Indeed, in geometry, these processes lie at the very core of making sense of problems and quantities (SMP 1 and 2), analyzing situations in ways that can be supported by viable arguments (SMP 3), communicating and thinking precisely (SMP 6), and looking for and making use of structure and regularity

(SMP 7 and 8). For instance, students can implement mathematical practice 7d, "Look for and make use of structure by seeing complicated things as single objects or being composed of several objects," only if they can analyze and decompose a complicated geometric object into a structured set of parts in which interrelationships between the parts are explicitly recognized, often through inferences drawn from formal properties. Instead of referring to CCSSM practices and NCTM Processes by number throughout the chapter, generally, reference will be made to the core mental processes described below.

- *Analyzing by decomposing.* Analyzing and reasoning about shapes by decomposing them into parts, making new wholes from parts, and knowing how the wholes and parts are related are crucially important in geometric reasoning and sense making (CCSSM practices: SMP 1a, 1b, 1f, 1g, 7a, 7d, 4c; NCTM Process Standards: PS1a, 1b, 3c, 4a, 4b, 5a, 5b).

- *Spatial structuring.* One of the CCSSM mathematical practices that is absolutely essential in geometric reasoning is looking for and using "structure." To *spatially structure* an object or set of objects is to mentally construct an organization or form for it by identifying its component parts and how they are spatially related, combining parts into bigger parts, and decomposing the shape into repeating smaller parts called composite units (CCSSM Practices: SMP 1a, 1b, 1g, 2a, 2b, 2c, 2d, 3b, 4a, 5d, 6a, 6b, 7a, 7b, 7d, 8b; NCTM Process Standards: PS 1a, 1b, 2a, 2b, 2c, 3a, 3c, 4a, 5a, 5b).

- *Coordinating spatial and quantitative processes.* Essential in geometric reasoning is coordinating spatial and quantitative reasoning, often coordinating spatial and numerical structuring. Indeed, in geometry, the meaning of numerical quantities comes from spatial analysis (CCSSM Practices: SMP 1a, 1b, 1d, 1f, 1g, 2a, 2b, 2c, 2d, 3a, 3b, 3c, 4a, 4b, 4c, 4d, 5a, 6b, 7a, 8a, 8b; NCTM Process Standards: PS 1a, 1b, 2a, 2b, 2c, 3a, 3b, 3c, 4a, 5a, 5b).

- *Using formal geometric concepts.* "Concepts organize experience" (Gelman and Kalish 2006, p. 1). Concepts are the building blocks of reasoning. In geometry, we use formal geometric concepts such as angle measure, length, parallelism, congruence, and transformations to analyze spatial phenomena. For instance, we use all these formal concepts to decompose a rectangular prism into opposite faces that are congruent rectangles (CCSSM Practices: SMP 1a, 1g, 2a, 2b, 2c, 2d, 3a, 6b, 7d; NCTM Process Standards: PS 2a, 3c, 4a, 5a, 5b).

Mental Models

Students' reasoning and sense making, and their use of the previously mentioned processes, are based on their mental models. *Mental models* are nonverbal image-like versions of situations that have the *structures* of the situations they represent. We understand or make sense of situations when we construct, activate, and manipulate mental models of the situations (Johnson-Laird 1983). For instance, we each have a mental model that enables us to navigate from our home to the school where we teach, to imagine things we might see along the route, and to determine detours if our normal route is blocked by construction. If mental models are sufficiently accurate and stable, we can mentally visualize moving around in them or moving, combining, and transforming objects in them, in the same way that we manipulate objects in the physical world. Mental models capture the meanings we construct for objects, and when we visualize, we are mentally operating on our mental models. We can help students develop proficiency with using geometric mental models by having them perform actions on shapes and reflect on those actions. Students develop visualization skills as they internalize acting and reflecting on physical objects, pictures, and visual animations.

The Close Relationship Between Spatial Structuring and Geometric Decomposition

Spatial structuring and geometric decomposition generally occur together. For instance, we distinguish different types of quadrilaterals by decomposing them into sides and angles and specifying their structure by describing relationships between their sides and/or angles (their properties). Parallelograms have pairs of *opposite sides equal*, whereas kites have pairs of *adjacent sides equal* (fig. 5.3a).

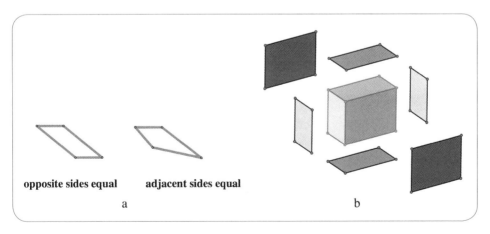

opposite sides equal   adjacent sides equal

a   b

Fig. 5.3

Similarly, we analyze and structure three-dimensional shapes by decomposing them into edges, vertices, and faces and noting their properties. For instance, we can characterize a right rectangular prism (a rectangular box) by decomposing it into its faces and edges and seeing that opposite faces are congruent rectangles and that all intersecting edges are perpendicular (fig. 5.3b).

Structuring and Quantification

Spatial structuring and geometric decomposition are also important because they underlie *meaningful* quantification and measurement of geometric objects (Battista 2012a). For instance, consider how students decompose and structure a 3-by-4-by-2–cube array into cubes (fig. 5.4a). Some students cannot mentally create a structure, so their mental model of the cube array is essentially a random set of cubes (fig. 5.4b). Other students incorrectly see the array only in terms of its faces (fig. 5.4c). Others structure the array correctly but irregularly (fig. 5.4d). Finally, some students structure the array into regular columns (fig. 5.4e) or, most efficiently, into layers (fig. 5.4f).

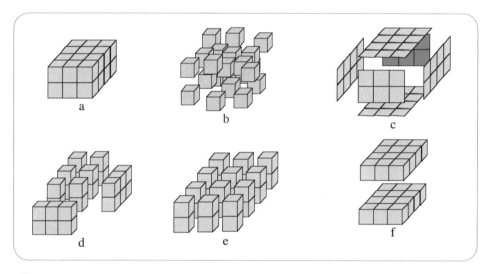

Fig. 5.4

The structure of students' mental models of cube arrays is a critical factor in determining how they enumerate the cubes in the arrays. The structurings depicted in figures 5.4b and 5.4c almost always lead to enumeration errors. In figure 5.4d the structuring is irregular so that, although it can help students correctly count the cubes in simple situations, it is not *generalizable* to larger arrays and is not easily described numerically. The column structuring in figure 5.4e is generalizable for cube arrays but does not lay the foundation for more sophisticated reasoning encountered later in mathematics. Only the layer structuring in figure 5.4f leads to efficient generalizable enumeration, easily helps students make sense of the volume formula, and lays a foundation for later reasoning. (As a useful exercise linking numeric and spatial structuring, teachers can ask students to explain how column structuring and layer structuring both can be used to give viable arguments justifying the volume formula for rectangular boxes.)

It is important to recognize that students in grades 3–5 have significant difficulties with cube enumeration problems. In one study of above-average students solving pictorially and concretely presented cube enumeration problems (Battista and Clements 1996), about 60 percent of the fifth graders but less than 20 percent of the third graders used a layered structuring. On the other hand, about 60 percent of third graders but only about 20 percent of fifth graders used a strategy that suggests that the students saw the arrays as consisting only of their outer faces (e.g., fig. 5.4c). Only 7 percent of third graders and 29 percent of fifth graders correctly used a layering strategy for all three problems.

Understanding Students' Mathematical Reasoning and Sense Making Using Learning Progressions

To make sense of the development of students' reasoning in a way that enables us to support their reasoning and sense making, learning progressions can be invaluable. For numerous mathematical topics, researchers have found that students' development of mathematical knowledge and reasoning can be characterized in terms of "levels of sophistication" (Battista 2011). A *level of sophistication* is a distinct type of conceptualizing and reasoning that occurs within a hierarchy of reasoning levels for a mathematical topic. A set of levels of sophistication forms a *learning progression*, which is a description of the successively more sophisticated ways of reasoning and sense making that students pass through in developing deep understanding of a topic.[5] Levels of sophistication can be thought of as mental plateaus that students ascend in a learning progression (fig. 5.5). Jumps between plateaus must be small enough so that students can achieve them with small amounts of instruction in relatively short periods of time.

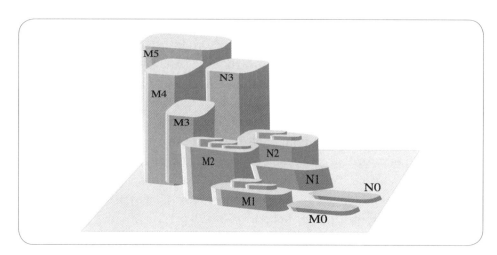

Fig. 5.5

Using learning progressions in teaching is important because once a student's reasoning about an idea has been located in a learning progression, the student's learning progress has been pinpointed and well-described, which provides the teacher with an excellent idea of where the student's reasoning development should proceed next to further promote his or her personal sense making about the topic. To effectively guide and support students' construction of meaning for specific mathematical topics, teachers and curriculum developers must understand how students construct meaning for those topics. Indeed, research shows that teachers who teach based on strong understanding of how students are constructing meaning for and reasoning about the mathematical topics they are teaching—using research-based learning progressions—teach in ways that improve student learning (Battista 2001; Bransford et al. 1999; Carpenter and Fennema 1991; Fennema and Franke 1992; Fennema et al. 1996).

We now examine learning progressions for students' reasoning for enumerating squares and cubes as needed in area and volume measurement. Although students' reasoning about volume lags behind their reasoning about area, the two progressions are described together to illustrate their common features.

Simplified Learning Progressions for Reasoning About Enumerating Area and Volume Units [6,7]

Level 1: Students Incorrectly Iterate Area- or Volume-Units

There are several types of reasoning that lead to incorrect iteration of area- and volume-units.

Incorrectly Locating Unit-Squares and Cubes

Area. See Katy's previously described work.

Volume. When asked how many cubes are needed to completely fill the box shown in figure 5.6, Bob counted the 8 cubes shown in the box, then pointed to and counted 6 imagined cubes on the box's left side, 4 on the back, 4 on the bottom, and 5 on the top. Bob's mental model of the cube array insufficiently located the cubes in it.

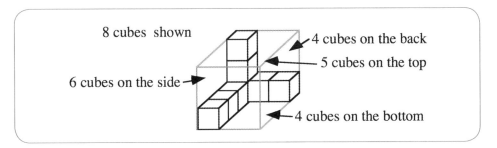

Fig. 5.6

Lack of Coordination in Area and Volume Measurement

To *coordinate* objects is to visualize or conceptualize how to place or arrange the objects relative to each other or to the whole of which they are parts (OED 2014). Many of the problems students have in reasoning about geometric objects stem from inadequate coordination.

Area. How many squares like this [*showing one plastic square*] does it take to cover this rectangle?

Bill: [*After correctly drawing the array of squares (fig. 5.7a), counts the 6 squares in the left column*] 1, 2, 3, 4, 5, 6. And so 6 here [*right column*]. That's 12. [*Counting the 4 squares on the top*] 1, 2, 3, 4. So 4 here [*bottom*]. That's 8 more, or 20. [*Counting the 8 squares in the middle*] 1, 2, 3, 4, 5, 6, 7, 8. So 28.

Because Bill did not coordinate the squares he saw in the top and bottom rows with those he saw in the right and left columns, he did not realize that he was double-counting the 4 corner squares.

Volume. Place a 4-by-4-by-3–cube building on a tabletop. Show a single cube. Ask, "How many of these cubes are in this building? The building is completely filled with the cubes. You can look at and touch the building, but you cannot take it apart."

Fred (fig. 5.7b) counted 12 cubes on the front, then immediately said there must be 12 on the back. He counted 16 on the top and immediately said there must be 16 on the bottom. Finally, he counted 12 cubes on the right side and immediately said there must be 12 on the left side. In each case, after counting the cubes visible on one side of the building, he correctly used a property of prisms—opposite faces congruent—to infer the number of cubes in the opposite side. However, Fred's strategy counted cubes on the edges and corners more than once. Because he did not properly coordinate what he saw on the different faces of the building, Fred failed to see when adjacent cube faces were part of the same cube.

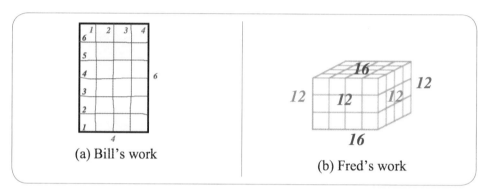

(a) Bill's work

(b) Fred's work

Fig. 5.7

Fred's difficulty is common among elementary and middle school students (Battista and Clements 1996). Research strongly suggests that lack of coordination in volume decomposition is a difficulty for a significant number of students in grades 3–8. Indeed, Ben-Chaim et al. (1985) reported data suggesting that about 39 percent of fifth to eighth graders double-counted cubes.

Starting the Transition to Level 2: Improved Coordination

A major breakthrough in reasoning occurs when students coordinate different perspectives on a square or cube array to create a mental model that recognizes when the same square or cube has already been counted. This refined mental model enables students to eliminate double-counting errors.

Area (continued from Bill in fig. 5.7a). When Bill explained his strategy to his teacher, he changed his mind. He then said there were 6 squares in each of the left and right columns, and counted 2 on the top, 2 on the bottom, and 8 in the middle. Through an increase in mental coordination, Bill realized that corner squares were part of rows and columns, and that to avoid double counting such squares, he could choose to count them as parts of sides but not as parts of the top and bottom.

Volume. As shown in figure 5.8, Juan coordinated spatial information sufficiently to avoid double counting edge cubes.

Juan: Well, there are 9 on the front [fig. 5.8]. So, that means there are 9 on the back. [*Pointing to the front column of the right side of the box picture*] These are the same blocks [as those already counted on the front], so you should only count the middle [*motioning along the middle two columns of the right side of the box picture*].

Juan: So we have 18; then 19, 20, 21, 22, 23, 24 [*counting cubes in the middle two columns on the right side of the box*]. And there are 6 more on the left side. That makes 30.

However, his conceptual coordination was still insufficient to build a mental model that properly located interior cubes; he thought that he had counted all the cubes needed to fill the box (missing the 6 cubes in the middle of the box).

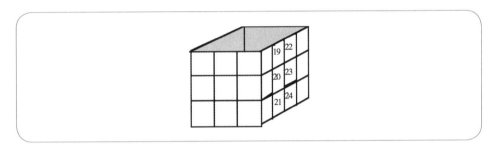

Fig. 5.8. Juan's work

Level 2: Students Correctly Iterate All Area- or Volume-Units One-By-One

This is the first level in which students' mental models correctly locate all squares or cubes in an array. However, although students sometimes obtain correct answers (as in the next two examples), because students inefficiently or inconsistently organize the units within arrays, they quite frequently lose their place in counting or adding and make enumeration errors. Furthermore, students' structuring and enumeration strategies are not generalizable and are inadequate for large arrays.

Area. David correctly located, structured, and counted the squares by ones in the rectangle in figure 5.9a.

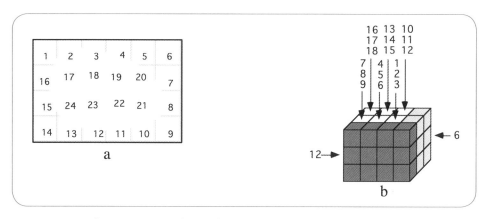

Fig. 5.9. Level 2 reasoning of David and Mary

Volume. Mary counted the cubes visible on the front face (12) then counted those on the right side that had not already been counted (6) (see fig. 5.9b). She then pointed to the remaining cubes on the top and counted cubes in columns of three: 1, 2, 3; 4, 5, 6, . . . 16, 17, 18. She then added 18, 12, and 6.

Level 3: Students Correctly Operate on Uniform Composites of Visible Area- or Volume-Units

When reasoning about visible arrays, students' mental models are structured to iterate the same composite unit throughout the enumeration process. At this level, however, students differ in the efficiency of the composites they iterate. The most efficient composites for area are rows and columns; the most efficient composites for volume are layers.

Less Efficient: Composites That Are Not Rows/Columns or Layers

Area. Billie correctly organized the array of squares in a 4-by-5 rectangle as composites of 2 squares.

Volume. Mary skip-counted by fours to enumerate column composites of cubes (fig. 5.10b).

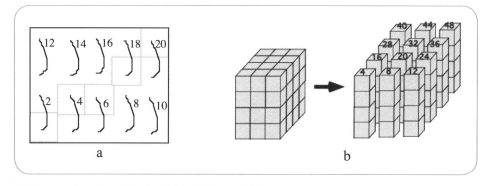

Fig. 5.10. Level 5: Work of (a) Billie and (b) Mary

More Efficient: Row/Column or Layer Composites

Area. Paul was shown that 5 plastic squares fit across the top of a rectangle and that 7 fit down the middle (then the squares were removed).

Paul: [*Counting and pointing across an imagined top row by ones*] 5 across; 7 down. [*Motioning across an imagined top 3 rows*] 5, 10, 15. [*Counting on seven fingers*] 5, 10, 15, 20, 25, 30, 35; 35.

Teacher: How did you know to stop at 35?

Paul: There are only 7 down that way [*motioning vertically down the middle of the rectangle*].

Volume. Students determine the number of cubes in a cube building by iterating layers as shown in figure 5.11. The layers can be vertical or horizontal, and students often use one of the sides of the cube building as a representation of a layer. Although some students who use layering count the cubes in a layer one-by-one, most enumerate the cubes using repeated addition, skip counting, or multiplication. (Mathematically, layer structuring is more general and powerful than utilizing the standard volume formula because it is also useful in thinking about the volumes of cylinders and even problems in calculus.)

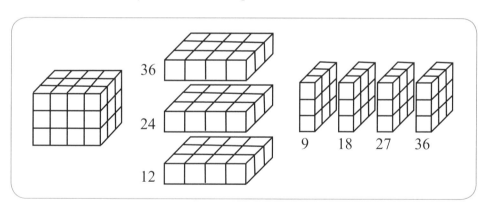

Fig. 5.11. Seeing buildings in terms of layers

Level 4. Students Correctly and Meaningfully Operate on Area-
or Volume-Units Using Only Numbers, and Explain Procedures
for Finding Areas and Volumes of Rectangular Objects

Area. Find the area of a rectangle that measures 10-by-12 inches.

Scott:	It's 10 times 12 equals 120 square inches.
Teacher:	Why did you multiply 10 times 12?
Scott:	Because there are 10 rows of 12 square inches.

Volume. Find the volume of a rectangular box that measures 5-by-10-by-3 inches.

Rita:	It's 5 times 10 times 3 equals 150 cubic inches.
Teacher:	Why did you multiply these three numbers together?
Rita:	Because 5 times 10 equals 50 cubic inches in one layer, and there are 3 layers, so it'd be 150 cubic inches.

Instructional Activities that Support Students' Movement Through the Learning Progressions[8]

The goal of instruction on area and volume should be to engage students with instructional tasks that encourage and support their movement through successively more sophisticated levels in the learning progressions previously described. Teachers help students develop personally meaningful reasoning not by "giving" them formulas but by giving them problems and encouraging them to invent, reflect on, test, and discuss strategies in a spirit of inquiry and problem solving using CCSSM Standards for Mathematical Practice, NCTM Process Standards, and the four basic mental processes that underlie them.

Teaching Area Measurement: Enumerating Squares in Rectangular Arrays

To construct proper mental models of two-dimensional arrays of squares, students need numerous opportunities to structure such arrays and to reflect on the appropriateness of their structurings. One good way of presenting such opportunities is to utilize, in inquiry-based instruction, problems similar to those already described. As you give students the rectangles (which should have dimensions in inches) provided in Appendix C, show students how a plastic inch-square fits exactly on one of the indicated squares. Students first predict how many squares are required to cover the rectangle then check their predictions with plastic squares.

Start with rectangles that give the most graphic information about the location of squares, then gradually move to rectangles that give less information (the rectangles in the appendix are listed roughly in this order). Give students several problems of each type so that they have an opportunity to develop adequate structuring for that type before moving on to more difficult problems. As a variation, after students have made their first prediction, have them draw how they think the plastic squares will cover the rectangle, make another prediction, then check their predictions with plastic squares. Many students will be able to make a correct prediction after drawing squares on a rectangle, but their structuring will not enable them to make a prediction without drawing. Students' explanations and drawings provide insights into their reasoning levels, information that can be invaluable in choosing appropriate instructional tasks, guiding discussions, and assessing student progress.

Teaching Volume Measurement: Enumerating Cubes in Boxes

Once students can accurately determine the number of cubes in buildings using actual cubes (at least when allowed to take the buildings apart), they can move on to activities like that shown in figure 5.12 (Battista and Berle-Carman 1996). The goal of this activity is to support students movement through the learning progression on cubes described above, arriving at mental models of cube arrays that are structured in ways that enable efficient enumeration of those arrays. To illustrate how students' reasoning progresses with appropriate instruction, a description of one typical student-pair's work on this activity follows (Battista 1999). The students' development of appropriate reasoning is not quick, but it is powerful.

A fifth-grade teacher distributed the How Many Cubes? activity sheet (fig. 5.12) to each student and explained that the students' goal was to find a way to correctly predict the number of cubes that fill boxes described by pictures, patterns, or words. Students worked collaboratively in pairs, predicting how many cubes would fit in a box then checking their answers by making the box out of grid paper and filling it with cubes. Students made predictions and checked their results for one problem before proceeding to the next.

How many cubes fit in each box? Predict; then build to check.
Check your prediction for a box before going on to the next box.

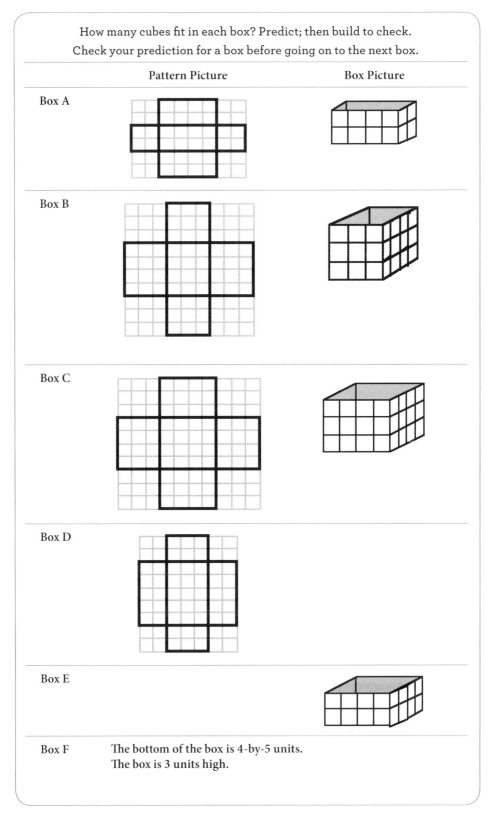

Fig. 5.12. How Many Cubes? activity (reduced size)

Box A. Nate counts the 12 outermost squares on the 4 side flaps of the pattern picture (see fig. 5.13); then he multiplies by 2. Pete counts the 12 visible cube faces on box picture A and then doubles that for the hidden lateral faces of the box. The boys agree on 24 as their prediction.

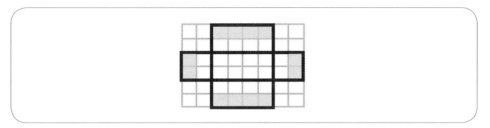

Fig. 5.13. The work of Nate and Pete for Box A

Pete:	[*After putting 4 rows of 4 cubes into box A*] We're wrong. It's 4 sets of 4 equals 16.
Nate:	What are we doing wrong? [*Neither student has an answer, so they move on to box B.*]
Pete:	[*Pointing at the 2 visible faces of the cube at the bottom right front corner of box picture B*] This is 1 box [cube], those 2.
Nate:	Oh, I know what we did wrong! We counted this [*pointing to the front face of the bottom right front cube*] and then the side over there [*pointing to the right face of that cube*].
Pete:	So we'll have to take away 4 [*pointing to the 4 vertical edges of box picture A*]. No, wait. We have to take away 8.

The discrepancy between Nate and Pete's predicted and actual answers for box A persuaded the two boys to reexamine their reasoning. When they reviewed Pete's strategy, they realized that he had mistakenly counted both the front and right faces of the same cube. That is, as the boys coordinated the positions of these faces, they recognized that these faces were the front and right faces of the same cube. This discovery was a critical milestone in the boys' movement through the learning progression.

Box B. In their prediction for box B, Pete counts 21 visible cube faces on the box picture, doubles it for the box's hidden lateral faces, then subtracts 8 for double counting (not taking into account that this box is 3 cubes high, not 2, like box A), predicting $42 - 8 = 34$. Nate adds 12 and 12 for the right and left lateral sides of box picture B, then 3 and 3 for the middle column of both the front and back, explaining that the outer columns of 3 on the front and back were counted when he enumerated the right and left faces. He predicts 30.

In their predictions for box B, Nate and Pete dealt with the double-counting error in different ways. Pete compensated for the error by subtracting the number of cubes he thought he had double-counted. He adjusted his original enumeration method by focusing on its numeric rather than spatial components. Nate attempted to visualize the cubes so that he would not double-count them. He focused on obtaining a properly structured mental model of the array. Unfortunately both boys had yet to properly structure the array.

After they construct box B, the boys use cubes to determine that it takes 36 cubes to fill it. This outcome puzzles them and causes them to reexamine the situation. Nate thinks that the error arose from missing interior cubes and tries to imagine the spatial organization of those cubes. Pete thinks the error arose from failing to properly account for the building height in his subtract-to-compensate-for-double-counting strategy, so he tries to figure out how to adjust his strategy numerically.

Box C. Nate and Pete jointly count 21 outside cube faces for box picture C, without double counting cubes on the right front vertical edge. They then multiply by 2 for the hidden back and left side and add 2 for the interior cubes (which is the number of cubes they concluded they had missed in the interior of box B). Their prediction is 44. The boys make and fill the box and find that it contains 48 cubes. They are puzzled.

As the boys reflect on their error, Pete concludes that they failed to count some of the cubes in the vertical edges. Again, as in his previous adjustments, Pete derives his correction by comparing the predicted and actual answers, not by finding an error in his spatial structuring. Nate deals with the error by continuing to focus on spatial structuring, and as a result, he makes a conceptual breakthrough on the next prediction—he moves to an even higher level in the learning progression.

Box D.

Nate: I think I know box D; I think it's going to be 30: 5 plus 5 plus 5 [*pointing to the columns in the pattern's middle*]: 15. And it's 2 high. Then you need to do 3 more rows of that, because you need to do the top: 20, 25, 30 [*pointing to the middle columns again*].

Box E. On the next problem (box picture E), because neither boy is able to employ Nate's layering strategy in this different graphic context, both return to variants of their old strategies, taking a step backward in their conceptualizing. However, after the boys complete the pattern for box E and fill it with cubes, Nate states that he believes his layering strategy would have worked.

Box F. Once the boys draw the pattern, Nate silently points to and counts the squares in its 4-by-5 middle section: 1–20 for the first layer, 21–40 for the second, and 41–60 for the third. The boys build the box and fill it with cubes to verify their answer. They are not at all surprised that they are correct; they were already sure of their answer.

After participating in two and a half one-hour sessions of small-group work, Nate, Pete, and their classmates arrived at a layer-based enumeration strategy that they could use in various situations (Battista 1999) and thereby moved from the lowest level of reasoning about cube arrays to meaningful enumeration reasoning at Level 4. Of course, this learning was not easy. Nate and Pete struggled to make sense of these ideas. But because they were accustomed to sense making in their mathematics class, they maintained their inquiry spirit until they developed a powerful way to reason about the volume problems that they were presented.

To help them extend their reasoning and sense making about cube arrays, the teacher gave the students in Nate and Pete's class the following decomposition problem. Brenda's journal entry clearly shows the decomposition reasoning she used to solve this problem. She decomposed the irregular shape into four rectangular prisms (fig. 5.14) so that she could apply the rectangular-box reasoning she had developed in the previous activity.

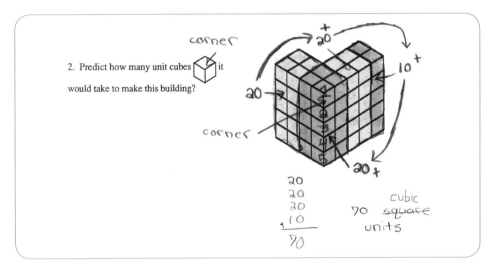

Fig. 5.14

The Predict-and-Check Approach

For the previously presented instructional activity and most of the others presented in this chapter, students should first make predictions, then check their predictions using concrete materials such as cubes and paper boxes. Predicting first is critical because students' predictions are based on their current ways of structuring the square/cube arrays. Making and testing predictions encourages students to reflect on and refine their structuring, helping them develop more powerful ways of conceptualizing and solving volume problems.

Having students merely fill rectangles with squares or fill boxes with cubes does not promote nearly as much productive student reflection because (a) the occurrence of discrepancies between predicted and actual answers that stimulate reorganization of thought is greatly reduced, and (b) students' attention is focused on physical activity rather than on their own thinking.

In working on volume problems with students in grades 3–5, especially with third graders, it is important to note that even when they are given a physical cube array, significant numbers of students have difficulty determining the number of cubes in the array if they cannot take the array apart. Indeed, Battista and Clements (1996) found that only 24 percent of above-average third graders and 63 percent of above-average fifth graders correctly solved a cube enumeration problem for which they could physically inspect the cube array but not take it apart. For such students, checking a prediction is not straightforward.

Transitioning to Higher-Level Reasoning About Area Decomposition

The next step in the development of students' reasoning about area is using decomposition and procedures for finding areas of rectangles to find areas of non-rectangular shapes. We will see how this progression occurs by following fourth grader Karen as she makes the transition from enumerating squares in rectangles to using decomposition to find areas of polygons (fig. 5.15). We begin by looking at her reasoning for finding areas of rectangles.

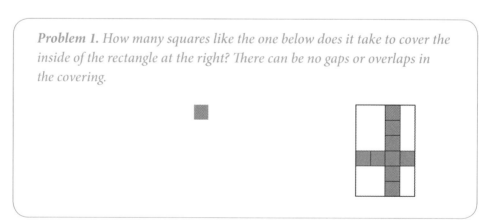

Problem 1. How many squares like the one below does it take to cover the inside of the rectangle at the right? There can be no gaps or overlaps in the covering.

Fig. 5.15

Karen: [*Motioning left to right across the squares in the displayed row of squares*] So there's 4 in each row [*points to each square in the displayed column*] 1, 2, 3, 4, 5, 6. There's 6 in each column [*moves from the top down in the displayed column, then up and* *back down again but to the right of the colum*n]. So there's 6, and there's 4 in here [*moves back and forth over the row*]. So I'm thinking that it's 6 times 4. And it would be 24.

Teacher: Why do you multiply 6 times 4?

Karen: Because if there's 6 in a column [*moves down and up the column*], and 4 in a row [*moves back and forth over row*], 6 times 4 is 24.

Karen used speech and gestures to help her make sense of the idea that if there are 6 squares in each column and 4 squares in each row in the rectangle, there are 4 columns of 6 squares, which means that you can multiply 6 times 4 for the total. So Karen was at Level 3 in the learning progression for area. To help Karen move to Level 4 reasoning, her teacher gave her several problems in which only the dimensions of rectangles were given (fig. 5.16a). To make sense of this problem in the new context, Karen had to be given the help page shown in figure 5.16b; she had to see squares.

Karen: [*Looking at the help page*] Oh, I see where the 7 and 6 come from now. They're how many squares are in rows and columns. So the area is just 7 times 6, which is 42.

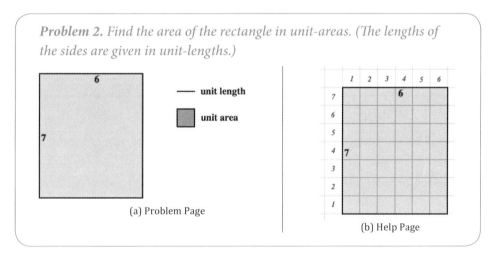

Problem 2. *Find the area of the rectangle in unit-areas. (The lengths of the sides are given in unit-lengths.)*

— unit length

▨ unit area

(a) Problem Page

(b) Help Page

Fig 5.16

After Karen successfully completed several additional problems like the one shown in figure 5.16a—without the aid of help pages—Karen's teacher had her move on to finding areas of polygons by decomposing the polygons into rectangles.

Problem 3. What is the area of the shaded polygon? Can using rectangles help you find the answer?

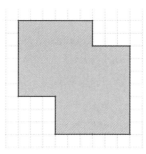

Fig. 5.17

| Karen: | Right here is kind of like a rectangle [*motioning along path 1 in figure 5.18*]. And right here is another rectangle [*motioning along path 2 then along paths 3–5 to make additional rectangles*]. |

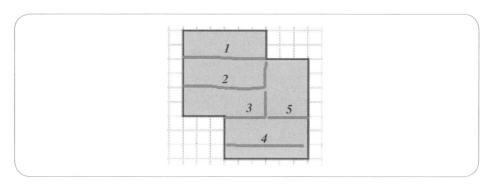

Fig. 5.18

| Karen: | So, all of these are mostly rectangles. So I can kind of see the squares but not really. But yeah, I can kind of see the lines . . . so maybe I can count them. |

Karen correctly decomposed the polygon into rectangles. However, she seemed to be thinking about counting squares instead of using the procedure she had developed for enumerating squares in single rectangles. But as she reflected on what she was doing, she came up with an alternate idea.

| Karen: | Oh, I have an idea what I can do. Because there's 1, 2, 3, 4, 5, 6 [*counts squares on the left side of the polygon (fig. 5.19a)*] in this row [actually a column]. |

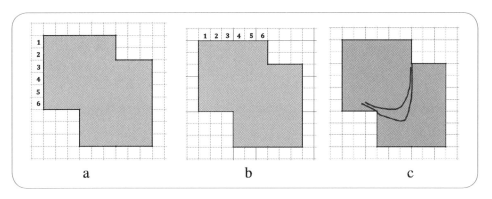

Fig. 5.19

Karen: So 1, 2, 3, 4, 5, 6 [*counts squares on the top of the polygon (fig. 5.19b)*]; so 6 times 6 is 36. And that takes care of this whole square [*motions to form a square (fig. 5.19c) and writes 36*]. Here I have an idea what I'm going to do. So 1, 2, 3 [*counts squares on the top right of the polygon (see fig. 5.20a)*]; so 3. Now 1, 2, 3, 4, 5, 6, 7 [*counts squares on the right side of the polygon (fig. 5.20b)*]; so 3 times 7 is 21.

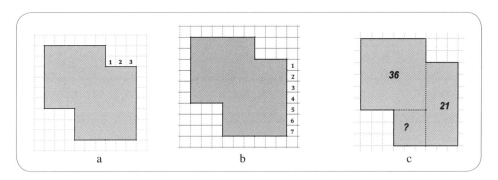

Fig. 5.20

Karen: So 36 plus 21 [*enters 36 + 21 into the calculator*] equals 57. So I think about 57 can fit in this.

Although Karen enumerated squares in rectangles correctly by using multiplication, *her decomposition of the polygon into rectangles was incorrect;* she did not include the area of the square with a question mark on it in figure 5.20c. Karen may have made one of two common errors that students make in multi-step geometry problems: (a) She may have lost track of where she was in her strategy, forgetting that she had not accounted for squares in the lower left corner; or, (b) she may have thought that the two rectangles she used actually did cover the whole polygon. Two good questions the teacher could have asked

Karen at this point are: "Do your two rectangles cover all the unit squares in the polygon?" and "Can you draw your two rectangles?" Rather than query her, the teacher gave Karen a hint page (see fig. 5.21) to examine.

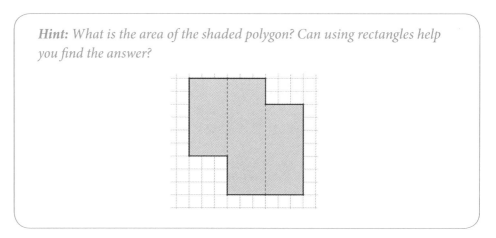

Hint: What is the area of the shaded polygon? Can using rectangles help you find the answer?

Fig.5.21

Karen: They did it a different way of how I did it. There's only 3 rectangles. So like in this rectangle [*motions to the left rectangle near the top (fig. 5.22a)*], there's 1, 2, 3. [*Counts squares on the left side of the left rectangle (fig. 5.22b)*]: 1, 2, 3, 4, 5, 6. So 3 times 6 is 18.

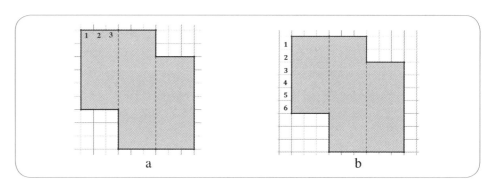

Fig. 5.22

Karen: And then there's [*counts squares across the top of the middle rectangle (fig. 5.23a)*] 1, 2, 3. [*Counts up the left side of the middle rectangle (fig. 5.23b)*]: 1, 2, 3, 4, 5, 6, 7, 8, 9; so 3 times 9 is 27. Then 27 plus 18 [*enters 27 + 18 into the calculator*] is 45.

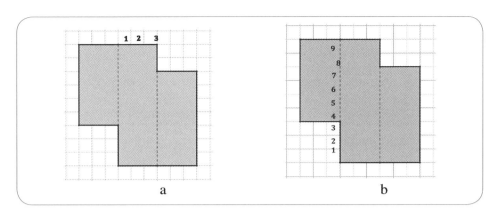

Fig. 5.23

Karen: So [*counts squares across the top of the right rectangle (fig. 5.24a)*]: 1, 2, 3. [*Continues counting squares on the right side of the right rectangle (fig. 5.24b)*]: 4, 5, 6, 7 [*pause*]. [*Re-counts squares on the right side of the right rectangle (fig. 5.24)c*]: 1, 2, 3, 4, 5, 6, 7. So 45 plus 21, because 3 times 7. [*Enters 21 + 45 into calculator*] 66 is a different answer than I got.

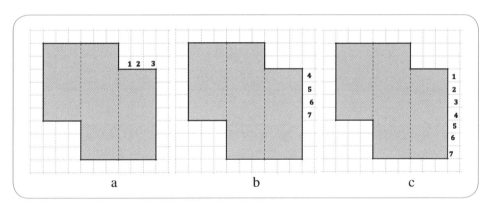

Fig. 5.24

Teacher: What do you think about this method?

Karen: [*Motioning on the rectangles*] I think that helped me a little bit more because of how they separated it up. Like I could tell 1, 2, 3 [*moves across the top of the left rectangle*], and there's 6 there [*moves down most of the left side of the left rectangle*].

Again, Karen was able to use multiplication to find the number of squares in rectangles after counting the squares on two adjacent sides of the rectangles. Note, however, that the counting she did for the rectangle on the right was initially incorrect, an error she might have made because she did not notice at first that her counting path went all the way around a corner. This suggests that her spatial structuring of arrays of rectangles was still a bit fragile. On the other hand, Karen did seem to understand the strategy of finding the area of the whole polygon by decomposing it into three rectangles and adding their areas.

Next Karen was given the same problem, except that this time it was not presented on a square grid (fig. 5.25). In this situation, Karen had to reason about rectangle areas using linear measurements.

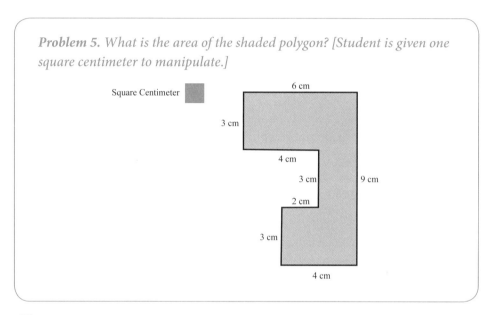

Problem 5. What is the area of the shaded polygon? [Student is given one square centimeter to manipulate.]

Square Centimeter

6 cm

3 cm

4 cm

3 cm

9 cm

2 cm

3 cm

4 cm

Figure 5.25

In this new context, Karen abandoned the strategy of decomposing the polygon into rectangles and multiplying length and width, and returned to a less sophisticated strategy of counting all unit-squares.

Karen: [*Moving the square centimeter as she counts*] So 1, 2, 3, 4, 5, 6 . . . 31, 32, 33. So I think it would be 33. [See fig. 5.26.]

Karen incorrectly counted squares because her structuring of the inside of the polygon was still fragile.

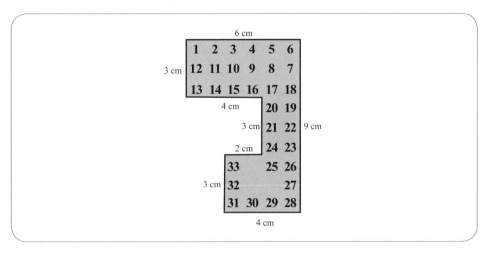

Fig. 5.26

Karen:	Or, what I could've done, well I could double-check my answer. . . . What I could also do is I could add all of these up [*motions around the perimeter of the polygon*]. [*Adds the side lengths on a calculator.*]
Teacher:	So what are you adding up?
Karen:	I'm adding up all of these numbers [*moves over most of the numbers on the perimeter*], and I think that would get me the answer. [*Enters the side lengths again into the calculator but adds an extra 3, getting 37.*] Um, I think I messed something up [*in her original solution of 33*]. I'm going to change my mind to 37.
Teacher:	You trust that method more than the other one [*counting squares*]?
Karen:	I think so. Yeah.

Inexplicably, Karen now adds side lengths to count squares. This indicates that she has either (a) resorted to a perimeter procedure she does not understand (many students confuse area and perimeter), or (b) failed in this more complex situation to understand the significance of the side lengths in the problem of enumerating squares to determine area. In the latter case, this means that she does not see that a side length tells her how many unit-squares fit along that length (even though she previously showed some understanding of this idea).

The teacher pursues both of these possibilities in the next episodes. First, hoping to better understand Karen's thinking and possibly enable Karen to see her error, the teacher gives Karen ten plastic centimeter squares (not enough to completely cover the polygon).

Karen: Okay, now I have more squares I can use. [*Drags the square centimeters and counts squares in the top rectangle as shown in figure 5.27*]: 1, 2, 3, . . . 17, 18.

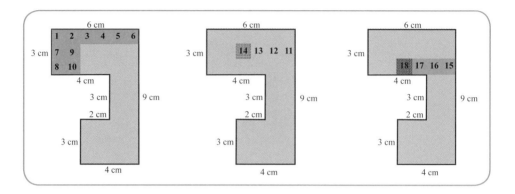

Fig. 5.27

Karen: Well, it's kind of confusing me, which ones I've done and which ones I haven't done. So, I think I'm going to trust my answer from last time with 37.

Teacher: And why do you trust that answer?

Karen: Because I added all of these up [*motions around the polygon*], and it's a square centimeter [*points toward a square centimeter*], and these are centimeters [*circles "6 cm" and "3 cm" on the top left*]. So, like 1, 2, 3 [*moves a square down along the left side labeled "3 cm" (fig. 5.28)*]; 3 squares can fit in there. So, I think that would be right.

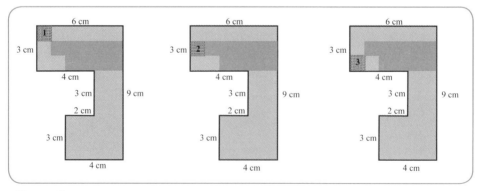

Fig. 5.28

Even though Karen understood that the "3 cm" label on the upper left side implies that three 1-centimeter squares fit along this side (addressing issue b above), she still believed that adding the side lengths would give her the area of the polygon. She did not even attempt to decompose the polygon into rectangles. So the teacher asked Karen to explain what area is.

Teacher: What is area? How do you find the area of a shape?

Karen: I think you find the number of squares it has.

Teacher: Is that what you were trying to do in this problem?

Karen: Yeah, finding squares.

Because Karen seemed to believe that her procedure of adding side lengths was giving her the number of squares in the polygon, the teacher returned to a previous context in which Karen's reasoning was correct: when the polygon was shown on a square grid.

Teacher: Okay. Suppose we put our shaded polygon on a square grid. And suppose we split it into rectangles. Does that help you? Can you double-check your answer?

Karen: Well, now I can count the squares. [*Correctly counts all the squares in the shape by ones.*] 36. I was close before.

Teacher: Can you use rectangles like you did before?

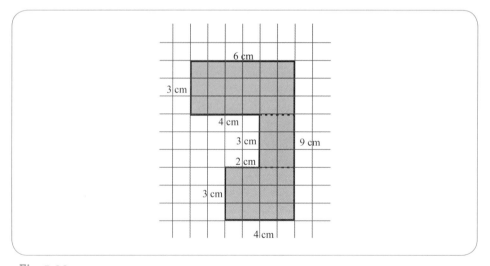

Fig. 5.29

Karen: Okay. [*Counts as shown in figure 5.30a*]: 1, 2, 3; then 1, 2, 3, 4, 5, 6. So 3 times 6 equals 18 [*writes 18*]. [*Counts as shown in figure 5.30b*]: 1, 2, 3; 1, 2. So 3 times 2 equals 6 [*writes 6*]. [*Counts as shown in figure 5.30c*]: 1, 2, 3; 1, 2, 3, 4. So 3 times 4 equals 12; 18 + 6 equals 24; and 24 + 12 equals 36. Same as when I counted the squares I could see inside.

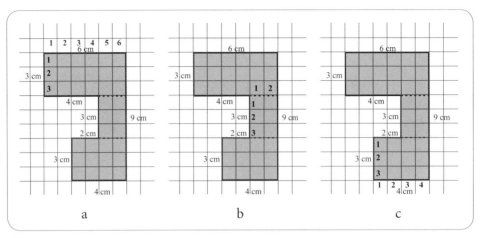

Fig. 5.30

When the teacher returned the problem to a grid context, Karen was able to correct her reasoning. Next the teacher tried to get Karen to use the side measurements directly, without counting, as Karen did earlier with rectangles. The teacher was trying to get Karen to apply Level 4 reasoning in the learning progression to decomposition problems.

Teacher: Is there any way you could have found out what to multiply without counting?

Karen: [*Counts squares along the sides of the top rectangle again (fig. 5.30a)*] Oh, it's 3 and 6, like here and here [*pointing to labeled side lengths*]. And down here [*pointing to labeled side lengths on the bottom rectangle*] maybe it's 3 and 4. [*Counting squares along the side lengths (fig. 5.30c)*] Yeah, that works. But you can't do that for the middle rectangle; you need to count the squares up and down: 1, 2, 3; 1, 2 [*counts squares as in figure 5.30b*].

Immediately after determining areas of rectangles in the larger figure by counting squares, Karen was able to see how to find the areas of rectangles in polygons using side measurements. Counting squares helped Karen to make sense of this procedure. But to solidify Karen's reasoning, she needed more tasks like the following one. This task begins with finding the area of a polygon with sides labeled like the one shown in figure 5.31a (students given this task should be provided with 18 plastic-unit squares). In the event that Karen were to need additional scaffolding, a hint page should be prepared (fig. 5.31b). First, Karen should do the problem as shown in figure 5.31a then she should check her answer with figure 5.31b. She should do more problems of this type until she can do them without the square grid page.

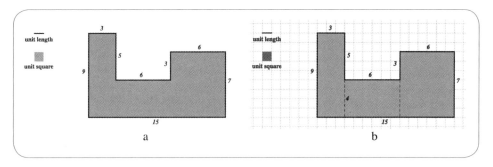

Fig. 5.31

At some point, instruction should also help Karen derive missing side lengths of polygons using properties of rectangles (equal opposite sides). For example, she should reason that she can derive the 4 on the left side of the dotted rectangle in figure 5.31b by subtracting 5 from 9.

Be Extremely Cautious About Teaching Area/Volume Formulas

The fact that Karen needed an "aha" moment to make sense of reasoning about area from side measurements is noteworthy; students do not move automatically from reasoning about area by iterating squares to reasoning about area by using linear measurements. Because taking this step in reasoning is a prerequisite to understanding the area formula for rectangles and thus reaching Level 4 in the learning progression for area, we must be very cautious about teaching this formula. It should be done only when students reach Level 3 reasoning. Similarly, given the research described in this chapter and elsewhere, we should reconsider the practice of teaching students to determine the number of cubes in a three-dimensional array by multiplying its length, width, and height before they have constructed a layer structuring of arrays, a practice found in mathematics textbooks for students as early as grade 3. The research suggests that only about 30 percent of fifth graders consistently mentally construct a layer structure for three-dimensional arrays, a construction that is absolutely necessary but certainly not sufficient for understanding such a procedure (Battista and Clements 1996).

But even for students who have mentally constructed layer structuring, it is questionable whether the procedure of multiplying the dimensions accurately describes the personally meaningful ways they have developed for finding the number of cubes in a box. Indeed, when students are given the volume-related instructional activities suggested in this chapter, almost all of them construct enumeration procedures that have two distinct steps: (1) determine the number of cubes in a layer (which students may or may not accomplish with multiplication); and (2) account for the number of layers (usually with multiplication, repeated addition, or skip counting). Even students who utilize multiplication for both steps do not usually describe their procedure using a three-factor product. For instance, two fifth graders wrote and described their general procedure for determining the number of cubes in a rectangular box as follows: They labeled the length A, the width B, and the height D, and said, "A times B equals C, that's the number on the bottom. C times D gives the total."

Thus, it is best to let students retain the procedure that almost all of them will develop if given appropriate instructional tasks: "Find out how many cubes are in a layer, then multiply by the number of layers." This student-generated procedure is not only personally meaningful to students but also much more powerful than the traditional formula because it generalizes to all prisms and can even form part of the conceptual basis for integral calculus.

Even when students routinely apply the procedure of multiplying length times width to find the areas of rectangles, we should give them assessments that probe the depth of their reasoning and sense making for this procedure. For instance, to examine students' understanding of the area formula for a rectangle and the way they connect the formula to spatial structuring (as applied to a single layer or cube packages), teachers gave students in grades 3–5 the following problem (see fig. 5.32) in a larger, one-page format. Teachers read the problem to the students while showing how an actual package made from 2 interlocking cubes fit into the paper box, with 5 packages along the length and 3 packages along the width. Students solved the problem, then provided written descriptions of how they did so.

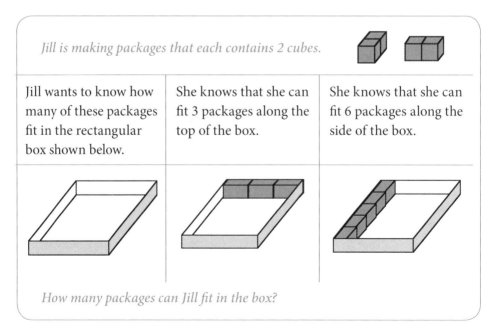

Jill is making packages that each contains 2 cubes.

Jill wants to know how many of these packages fit in the rectangular box shown below.	She knows that she can fit 3 packages along the top of the box.	She knows that she can fit 6 packages along the side of the box.

How many packages can Jill fit in the box?

Fig. 5.32

As table 5.1 shows, intermediate students who were given this problem performed very poorly. The most prevalent error was their rote use of the formula/procedure for the area of a rectangle, "length times width," which led to an answer of 15.

Table 5.1. Percentage of students giving each type of answer for the problem in figure 5.32 (Battista 1998)

Answer	Grade 3 (80 students)	Grade 4 (93 students)	Grade 5 (117 students)
Correct [30]	4	10	9
Incorrect			
15	41	53	64
Other	55	37	27

The work of some students indicated that their thinking about the formula was not connected to a properly structured mental model of how the packages fit into the box. They structured the box as either 3 columns of 5 packages or 5 rows of 3 packages without recognizing how the packages actually fit in the box (see fig. 5.33).

John: We know 3 will fit across, and we know 5 will fit downward, so just multiply.

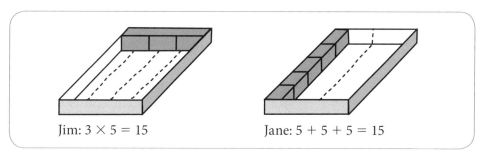

Jim: $3 \times 5 = 15$ Jane: $5 + 5 + 5 = 15$

Fig. 5.33

Less than 10 percent of students in grades 3–5 were able to use the given information in this problem to create a mental model that accurately structured the packages in the box. And the percentage of students who incorrectly applied the area formula—a clear indication that the formula was learned rotely—actually increased as the grade level rose. Almost 90 percent of the students used inadequate spatial structuring in their reasoning and sense making about the problem.

This is a great assessment task to give to students to help them reason more deeply and truly make sense of the area formula. We already know that given physical cube-packages and boxes, most students can figure out an appropriate structuring of the packages and properly relate this structuring to the computation 5 times 6 equals 30. To help the students create an accurate mental model, first present the problem to the class as previously described. Next, have students build the box from a pattern you supply; then use interlocking cubes to test their answers. For students who use the formula, ask: "Why does multiplying 5 times 3 NOT work here? But why does this procedure work for finding area using unit-squares?"

Meaningful Use of Linear Measurements

Discussion of the problem in figure 5.32 is another way to help students make sense of how exactly we use linear measurements in area and volume procedures (recall the earlier discussion of how Karen made sense of this idea for the area of rectangles). It is only when students can properly structure and enumerate squares in two-dimensional arrays or cubes in three-dimensional arrays (Level 3) that they should explore what *linear measurements* reveal about these arrays. For instance, show students an unmarked rectangle, tell them it is 5 cm wide and 8 cm long, and ask: "What is the area of the rectangle in square centimeters? Exactly how and why can length measurements be used to find the number of square centimeters that cover a rectangle?" Be sure that students clearly distinguish length and area units. Similarly, for volume, students can be asked to find the number of cubic centimeters that fit in a closed, unmarked, rectangular box with measurements of 5, 6, and 4 cm.

Conclusion

This chapter has illustrated how students can develop powerful, structured, and adaptive reasoning and sense making about geometric decomposition in reasoning about area and volume (as well as how they often fail to do so). It has also illustrated how teachers can use knowledge of students' reasoning, including learning progressions, to guide their choice of instructional activities and instructional interactions with students. Designing and implementing instruction that supports students' meaningful learning of area and volume measurement—including geometric decomposition—must be based on a firm understanding of the learning progressions that describe the development of students' reasoning about these concepts. Such understanding is essential to teaching in a way that is consistent with professional recommendations and modern research on students' mathematics learning. Instruction based on such understanding provides students with great opportunities to truly succeed in genuine geometric reasoning and sense making.

The examples described in this chapter also indicate that students frequently determine geometric decompositions—like that required to enumerate the number of unit-areas or -volumes—without paying sufficient attention to the process of spatial structuring. They employ numerical operations that are insufficiently connected to the spatial reasoning that makes these operations truly meaningful. Elementary students do this because most of them are unaware of the critical role that spatial structuring plays in dealing with geometry problems. It is no wonder that so many of them make structuring errors in area and volume problems; it does not occur to most of them to look carefully at how they might structure the situations. Others have had so few opportunities to reason about structuring arrays that they have little understanding of, or skill with, this critical process. Thus, if we want to increase the power of students' geometric-measure reasoning and sense making, we must provide them with numerous opportunities to develop their spatial structuring skills.

Notes

1. Much of my research and development referenced in this chapter was supported in part by the National Science Foundation under grant numbers 0099047, 0352898, 554470, 838137, and 1119034. The opinions, findings, conclusions, and recommendations, however, are mine and do not necessarily reflect the views of the National Science Foundation.

2. These are sobering findings, given that for many students in these grades, traditional instruction uses rectangular arrays as one model to *give* meaning to multiplication, assuming that students see such arrays as sets of equivalent columns and rows.

3. I have discussed learning progressions, assessment, and related instructional activities for other geometry topics in numerous publications (Battista 2003, 2007ab, 2009, 2012ab).

4. A numbered/lettered summary of the CCSM Mathematical Practices and NCTM Process Standards is given in the Appendix.

5. It is assumed that all students pass through almost all of the levels in learning progressions. What varies is the speed at which they pass through the levels and the amount of instructional scaffolding students need to pass through each level. Also, during the learning process, students might be at different levels for different categories of problems.

6. Area and volume are discussed together to emphasize common mental processes and difficulties. However, the levels for enumerating cubes typically lag behind the levels for squares by about two years.

7. Much more extensive discussions of the learning progressions for area and volume can be found in Battista 2012.

8. Additional information on instruction can be found in Akers et al. 1997, Battista and Clements 1995, Battista and Berle-Carman 1996, and Battista 2012.

References

Akers, J., M. T. Battista, A. Goodrow, D. H. Clements, and J. Sarama. *Shapes, Halves, and Symmetry.* Palo Alto, Ca.: Dale Seymour Publications, 1997.

Battista, M.T. "How Many Blocks." *Mathematics Teaching in the Middle School* 3, no. 6 (1998): 404–411.

Battista, M. T. "The Importance of Spatial Structuring in Geometric Reasoning." *Teaching Children Mathematics* 6, no. 3 (1999): 170–177.

Battista, M. T. "How Do Children Learn Mathematics? Research and Reform in Mathematics Education." In *The Great Curriculum Debate: How Should We Teach Reading and Math?* edited by Thomas Loveless, pp. 42–84. Brookings Press, 2001.

Battista, M. T. *Shape Makers: Developing Geometric Reasoning in the Middle School with the Geometer's Sketchpad.* Berkeley, Ca.: Key Curriculum Press, 2003.

Battista, M. T. "Understanding Students' Thinking About Area and Volume Measurement." In *2003 Yearbook, Learning and Teaching Measurement,* edited by D. H. Clements, pp. 122–142. Reston, Va.: National Council of Teachers of Mathematics, 2003.

Battista, M. T. "The Development of Geometric and Spatial Thinking." In Second Handbook of Research on Mathematics Teaching and Learning, edited by F. Lester, pp. 843–908. Reston, Va.: National Council of Teachers of Mathematics, 2007a.

Battista, M. T. "Learning with Understanding: Principles and Processes in the Construction of Geometric Ideas." In 69th NCTM Yearbook, The Learning of Mathematics, edited by M. E. Strutchens and W. G. Martin, pp. 65–79. Reston, Va.: National Council of Teachers of Mathematics, 2007b.

Battista, M. T. "Highlights of Research on Learning School Geometry." In *2009 Yearbook, Understanding Geometry for a Changing World,* edited by T. Craine and R. Rubenstein, pp. 91–108. Reston, Va.: National Council of Teachers of Mathematics, 2009.

Battista, M. T, "Fifth Graders' Enumeration of Cubes in 3D Arrays: Conceptual Progress in an Inquiry-based Classroom." *Journal for Research in Mathematics Education* 30, no. 44 (July 1999): 17–48.

Battista, M. T. "Conceptualizations and Issues Related to Learning Progressions, Learning Trajectories, and Levels of Sophistication." *The Mathematics Enthusiast* 8, no. 3 (2011): 506–569.

Battista, M. T., and M. Berle-Carman. *Containers and Cubes.* Palo Alto, Ca.: Dale Seymour Publications, 1996.

Battista, M. T., and D. H. Clements. "Students' Understanding of Three-Dimensional Rectangular Arrays of Cubes." *Journal for Research in Mathematics Education* 27 (May 1996): 258–292.

Battista, Michael T. *Cognition-Based Assessment and Teaching of Geometric Measurement (Length, Area, and Volume): Building on Students' Reasoning.* Portsmouth, N.H.: Heinemann, 2012a.

Battista, Michael T. *Cognition-Based Assessment and Teaching of Geometric Shapes: Building on Students' Reasoning.* Portsmouth, N.H.: Heinemann, 2012b.

Battista, Michael T. "Fifth Graders' Enumeration of Cubes in 3d Arrays: Conceptual Progress in an Inquiry-Based Classroom." *Journal for Research in Mathematics Education* 30 (July 1999): 417–448.

Battista, Michael T., Douglas H. Clements, Judy Arnoff, Kathryn Battista, and Caroline V. A. Borrow. "Students' Spatial Structuring and Enumeration of 2D Arrays of Squares." *Journal for Research in Mathematics Education* 29 (November 1998): 503–532.

Battista, Michael T., and Douglas H. Clements. *Exploring Solids and Boxes.* Palo Alto, Ca.: Dale Seymour Publications, 1995.

Ben-Chaim, D., G. Lappan, and R. T. Houang. "Visualizing Rectangular Solids Made of Small Cubes: Analyzing and Effecting Students' Performance." *Educational Studies in Mathematics 16* (1985): 389–409.

Bransford, J. D., A. L. Brown, and R. R. Cocking. *How People Learn: Brain, Mind, Experience, and School.* Washington, D.C.: National Research Council, 1999.

Carpenter, T. P., and E. Fennema. "Research and cognitively guided instruction." In *Integrating Research on Teaching and Learning Mathematics*, edited by E. Fennema, T. P. Carpenter, and S. J. Lamon, pp. 1–16. Albany, N.Y.: State University of New York Press, 1991.

Clements, D. H., and J. Sarama. (2009). *Learning and Teaching Early Math: The Learning Trajectories Approach.* New York: Routledge, 2009.

Fennema, E., and M. L. Franke, M. L. "Teachers' Knowledge and Its Impact." In *Handbook of Research on Mathematics Teaching,* edited by D. A. Grouws, pp. 127–164. Reston, Va.: National Council of Teachers of Mathematics/Macmillan, 1992.

Fennema, E., T. P. Carpenter, M. L. Franke, L. Levi , V. R. Jacobs, and S. B. Empson. "A Longitudinal Study of Learning to Use Children's Thinking in Mathematics Instruction." *Journal for Research in Mathematics Education* 27, no. 4 (1996): 403–434.

Gelman, S. A., and C. W. Kalisch. (2006). Conceptual Development. In *Handbook of Child Psychology: Vol 2, Cognition, perception, and language.* 687–733.

Hirstein, J. J. "The Second National Assessment in Mathematics: Area and Volume." *Mathematics Teacher 74* (1981): 704–708.

Johnson-Laird, P. N. *Mental Models: Towards a Cognitive Science of Language, Inference, and Consciousness.* Cambridge, Ma.: Harvard University Press, 1983.

Lappan, G., J. T. Fey, and E. F. Phillips. *Ruins of Montarek: Spatial Visualization (Connected Mathematics Series).* Palo Alto, Ca.: Dale Seymour Publications, 1998.

National Council of Teachers of Mathematics. *Principles and Standards for School Mathematics.* Reston, Va.: National Council of Teachers of Mathematics, 2000.

National Research Council (NRC). *Learning To Think Spatially.* Washington, D.C.: National Academy Press, 2006.

Newcombe, N. S. "Picture This." *American Educator* (2010): 28–35.

Outhred, L., and M. Mitchelmore. "Young Children's Intuitive Understanding of Rectangular Area Measurement. *Journal for Research in Mathematics Education* 31, no. 2 (2000): 144–167.

Sarama, J., and D. H. Clements. *Early Childhood Mathematics Education Research: Learning Trajectories for Young Children.* New York: Routledge, 2009.

Wai, J., D. Lubinski, and C. P. Benbow. "Spatial Ability for STEM Domains: Aligning over 50 Years of Cumulative Psychological Knowledge Solidifies Its Importance. *Journal of Educational Psychology* 101, no. 4 (2009): 817–835.

Wheatley, C. L., and G. H. Wheatley, "Developing Spatial Ability." *Mathematics in School* 8, no. 1 (1979): 10–11.

Appendix

Rectangle Tasks

a	b	c	d

e	f	g	h

i	j	k
	Students are shown that 4 square tiles go across the top (then the tiles were removed), and that 3 square tiles go down the middle (then the tiles were removed).	Students are shown that 5 square tiles go across the top (then the tiles were removed), and that 7 square tiles go down the middle (then the tiles were removed).

APPENDIX A

Abbreviated List of the *Common Core State Standards for Mathematics*

Standards for Mathematical Practice

1. ***Make sense of problems and persevere in solving them.***

   a. Seriously attempt to grasp the meaning of a problem.

   b. Analyze givens, constraints, relationships, and the form and meaning of solutions.

   c. Plan a solution pathway rather than simply jumping into a solution attempt.

   d. Consider analogous problems, and try special cases and simpler problems, looking for insight.

   e. Monitor and evaluate progress, and check answers using different methods.

   f. Translate between different representations.

   g. Continually ask, "Does this make sense?"

   h. Understand other approaches.

   i. Draw diagrams of important features and relationships.

2. ***Reason abstractly and quantitatively.***

   a. Make sense of quantities and their relationships.

   b. Decontextualize—abstract a given situation, represent it symbolically, and manipulate symbols without necessarily attending to their referents.

c. Contextualize—pause during the manipulation process to reflect on referents for symbol manipulations.

d. Create a coherent representation; consider the units involved; attend to the meaning of quantities; and know and flexibly use different properties of operations and objects.

3. *Construct viable arguments and critique the reasoning of others.*

   a. Understand and use assumptions, definitions, and previously established results in constructing arguments.

   b. Make conjectures and build a logical progression of statements to explore the truth of conjectures.

   c. Analyze situations by breaking them into cases, and recognize and use counterexamples.

   d. Justify conclusions, communicate them to others, and understand and evaluate the arguments of others.

   e. Reason inductively about data, making plausible arguments that take into account the context from which the data arose.

   f. Compare the effectiveness of plausible arguments, distinguish correct logic or reasoning from that which is flawed, and—if there is a flaw in an argument—explain what it is.

   g. Elementary students can construct arguments using concrete referents such as objects, drawings, diagrams, and actions.

4. *Model with mathematics.*

   a. Apply mathematics to solve real-world problems. [In early grades, this might be as simple as writing an addition equation to describe a situation.]

   b. Make appropriate assumptions and approximations to simplify a complicated situation, realizing that these may need revision.

   c. Identify important quantities in a practical situation and interconnect their relationships.

   d. Interpret mathematical results in the context of the situation and reflect on whether the results make sense.

5. *Use appropriate tools strategically.*

   a. Consider and evaluate the usefulness of various available tools (including technology) when solving a mathematical problem.

   b. Make sound decisions about when various tools might be helpful, recognizing both the insight to be gained and their limitations.

    c. Detect possible errors by strategically using estimation and other mathematical knowledge.

    d. Use technological tools to explore and deepen understanding of concepts.

6. *Attend to precision.*

    a. Communicate precisely to others.

    b. Use clear definitions in own reasoning and in discussion with others.

    c. State the meanings of symbols and representations chosen, and use symbols, including the equal sign, consistently and appropriately.

    d. Calculate accurately and efficiently; express numerical answers with a degree of precision appropriate for the problem context.

    e. In the elementary grades, students give carefully formulated explanations to each other. By the time they reach high school they have learned to examine claims and make explicit use of definitions.

7. *Look for and make use of structure.*

    a. Look closely to discern a pattern or structure (like noticing that arithmetic computations satisfy the commutative or distributive property or that a set of figures all have four sides).

    b. Recognize the significance of an existing line in a geometric figure and use the strategy of drawing an auxiliary line for solving problems.

    c. Step back for an overview and shift perspective.

    d. See complicated things as single objects or as being composed of several objects.

8. *Look for and express regularity in repeated reasoning.*

    a. Notice if calculations are repeated, and look both for general methods and shortcuts.

    b. Notice regularity.

    c. In problem solving, maintain oversight of the process while attending to the details.

    d. Continually evaluate the reasonableness of intermediate results.

Note: You can access and download this appendix online by visiting NCTM's More4U website (nctm.org/more4u). The access code can be found on the title page of this book.

Appendix B

Abbreviated List of National Council of Teachers of Mathematics Principles and Standards for School Mathematics

Process Standards

1. ***Problem Solving***

   a. Solve problems using a variety of appropriate strategies while monitoring and reflecting on the problem-solving process.

   b. Build new mathematical knowledge through problem solving.

2. ***Reasoning and Proof***

   a. Use various types of reasoning and proof, and recognize reasoning and justification as fundamental to mathematics.

   b. Make and investigate mathematical conjectures.

   c. Develop and evaluate mathematical arguments.

3. ***Communication***

   a. Organize, consolidate, and communicate mathematical thinking coherently and clearly.

   b. Analyze and evaluate mathematical thinking and strategies.

   c. Use the language and concepts of mathematics to express mathematical ideas precisely.

4. ***Connections***

   a. Interconnect mathematical ideas.

   b. Apply mathematics in contexts outside of mathematics.

5. *Representation*

    a. Create and use representations to organize, reason, and problem solve as well as record and communicate mathematical ideas.

    b. Translate among mathematical representations.

Note: You can access and download this appendix online by visiting NCTM's More4U website (nctm.org/more4u). The access code can be found on the title page of this book.